Luna Gale

Rebecca Gilman's plays include *Boy Gets Girl, Spinning into Butter, Blue Surge, The Glory of Living, The Sweetest Swing in Baseball, The Heart Is a Lonely Hunter, Dollhouse* and *The Crowd You're in With.* Among her many awards have been a Guggenheim Fellowship, the Harold and Mimi Steinberg/ATCA New Play Award, the Harper Lee Award, the Scott McPherson Award, the Prince Prize for Commissioning New Work, the Roger L. Stevens Award, the *Evening Standard* Award for Most Promising Playwright, and the George Devine Award. *Boy Gets Girl* received an Olivier nomination for Best New Play and she was a finalist for the 2001 Pulitzer Prize for *The Glory of Living.* She received her MFA in playwriting from the University of Iowa and is an associate professor of playwriting and screenwriting at Northwestern University. She is an Artistic Associate at the Goodman Theatre, Chicago, where *Luna Gale* received its world premiere in 2014.

by the same author from Faber

BOY GETS GIRL
SPINNING INTO BUTTER
THE GLORY OF LIVING
THE SWEETEST SWING IN BASEBALL

REBECCA GILMAN

Luna Gale

FABER & FABER

First published in 2015
by Faber and Faber Ltd
74–77 Great Russell Street
London WC1B 3DA

Typeset by Country Setting, Kingsdown, Kent CT14 8ES
Printed in England by CPI Group (UK) Ltd, Croydon CR0 4YY

A CIP record for this book
is available from the British Library

978-0-571-32742-3

2 4 6 8 10 9 7 5 3 1

Luna Gale received its World Premiere at the Goodman Theatre, Chicago, Illinois (Robert Falls, artistic director; Roche Schulfer, executive director), on 27 January 2014. The cast, in alphabetical order, was as follows:

Cindy Jordan Baker
Karlie Reyna de Courcy
Lourdes Melissa DuPrey
Caroline Mary Beth Fisher
Cliff Erik Hellman
Peter Colin Sphar
Pastor Jay Richard Thieriot

Directed by Robert Falls
Sets by Todd Rosenthal
Costumes by Kaye Voyce
Lighting by Robert Wierzel
Music and sound by Richard Woodbury

Luna Gale was first presented in London on Hampstead Theatre's Main Stage on 13 June 2015. The cast, in alphabetical order, was as follows:

Peter Alexander Arnold
Cindy Caroline Faber
Cliff Ed Hughes
Pastor Jay Corey Johnson
Karlie Rachel Redford
Lourdes Abigail Rose
Caroline Sharon Small

Director Michael Attenborough
Designer Lucy Osborne
Lighting Jon Clark
Sound John Leonard
Casting Joyce Nettles

Characters

Caroline
fifty

Karlie
nineteen

Peter
nineteen

Cindy
forty

Lourdes
eighteen

Cliff
thirty-five

Pastor Jay
late thirties

Place: Cedar Rapids, Iowa

Time: the present

Act One

A small waiting room at a hospital. Six or eight chairs; the type that are attached by a rod and bolted to the floor. Hospital colours. A fake plant. A framed, faded poster of a lighthouse.

A door leads into the examination rooms. It has a small window in it, but it is locked. There is a keypad on the wall next to the door.

Karlie and Peter, both nineteen, sit in the chairs upstage. Peter is dressed in cargo shorts and a T-shirt. He is slumped forward in his chair, asleep or semi-conscious. All of his fingers have Band-Aids wrapped round the tips.

Karlie – jeans, tank top, tattoos, pink or blue highlights in her hair and black nail polish – is very upright. On the floor next to her is her giant bag. It is open at the top. One move and everything will tumble out of it.

Karlie is eating a piece of cheesecake from a clear, plastic, take-out container. It has a cherry topping. There is a quick, steady rhythm to the way she stabs a piece of cheesecake with the plastic fork, puts it in her mouth, chews, then stabs another. She is not savouring her food, nor is she inhaling it. She is feeding the machine with fuel. While she eats, and throughout, her knee jerks up and down with an insane, nervous energy.

Suddenly, she is distracted. She sees a bag of Skittles in her open bag.

Karlie Do you want some Skittles?

She drops the cheesecake on the floor and picks up the Skittles. Peter does not move.

Yo. Skittles?

She pours out a handful and nudges him.

Dude. Come on.

She nudges him again. He groans.

You should eat.

She puts them under his nose.

You'll feel better. Dude. Eat.

Barely opening his eyes, he takes the handful of Skittles and shoves them in his mouth.

Chew. Chew!

He chews.

Thank you.

She pours out some more Skittles and jams them in her mouth. Then she jumps up and looks through the window on the door.

Ughh. What's the fucking deal? We've been here three hours. Emergency room.

She bangs on the door twice, with each syllable.

E-mer-gen-cy room!

Bangs.

Hello!

She sees the keypad.

What if like –

She starts punching keys and making electronic beeping noises.

Beep beep beep beep beep beep boop. Open up. Open up.

Looks through the window again. Yells.

Does anybody even work here?!

From her pocket comes the ring of a cell phone. She looks at the number, answers it.

What?

Beat.

No! I'm still in the fucking emergency room.

Beat.

Because I have it written down on a piece of paper at home but I am in the emergency room at the hospital. Can you comprehend that?

Beat.

Three hours! They just left us sitting in this goddamn room that's supposedly the expediting room? Like this was the room where things would happen, but we're just fucking –

Yells.

SITTING HERE –

Normal.

– and nobody will tell us –

Yells.

– WHAT'S HAPPENING.

Beat.

I don't have his number.

Beat.

Because.

I didn't programme it into my phone because I never want to call him again because last time I saw him was at the Kum and Go and he was microwaving a burrito and I didn't even want anything, I just asked him what's up and he's like, 'Don't even talk to me if you don't have the cash.'

Beat. Suddenly sober.

Then go to his apartment because that's serious, if that's what's happening that's serious.

Peter, without lifting his head, puts his hand out, palm up. Karlie sees and pours him some more Skittles.

You have to take the Five-A. Catch it at the hub, it only goes one direction from there.

During this, Caroline, fifty, enters. She is sensibly dressed for June in Iowa. She carries a patient file. Karlie doesn't notice her.

I can't remember the stop but it's the one right when you see the Hy-Vee –

Caroline Karlie?

Karlie (*on phone*) I don't know. First floor at the far end –

Caroline (*louder*) Karlie Quinn?

Karlie (*suddenly alert to Caroline*) What? What is it?

Caroline Are you Luna's mother?

Karlie (*hangs up the phone*) Is she okay?

Caroline You're Luna's mom?

Karlie What's going on?

Caroline They're giving her intravenous fluids. She's severely dehydrated.

Karlie Is she going to be okay?

Caroline (*indicating Peter, who has dropped back to sleep*) Is this Luna's dad?

Karlie Yes.

Shoves Peter.

Wake up.

Peter groans.

Wake up!

Peter lifts his head.

Caroline How long has Luna had diarrhoea?

Karlie Like, two days.

Caroline (*looks at the chart*) You told Admitting that it started this morning.

Karlie No, like two days ago it was loose, then she had a regular b.m. yesterday morning? Then I don't know what it was yesterday but when I got home from work last night it was loose again –

Her phone starts to ring.

Stupid – shut up!

She silences it.

Caroline Loose or watery?

Karlie Yeah.

Peter's head drops again. Karlie shoves him.

Wake up, asshole!

Caroline What's his name?

Karlie Peter.

Caroline What's wrong with him?

Karlie Nothing.

Shoves him.

The nurse is here. Wake up.

Peter wakes up. Sort of.

So can we see her?

Caroline Not right now.

Karlie Why not?

Caroline (*looks at the remains of the cheesecake*) Was somebody eating cheesecake?

Karlie Me. I mean, no. It was all they had in the cafeteria.

Caroline And Skittles. And . . .

Looks in Karlie's open bag.

Starburst. And Fruit Runts. And SweetTarts.

Karlie What?

Caroline That's a lot of sugar.

Karlie When can we see her?

Caroline What happened to Peter's fingers?

Beat.

Karlie Nothing.

Caroline Then why all the Band-Aids?

Karlie You're not a nurse, are you?

Caroline I'm with the Department of Human Services –

Karlie You're a fucking social worker.

Caroline Luna's been sick for a while, hasn't she?

Karlie Just since Monday.

Caroline So four days.

Karlie One.

Caroline Today's Thursday.

Karlie Today's Tuesday.

Caroline Today's Thursday. How long have the two of you been smoking meth?

No answer.

Karlie?

Karlie I want to see Luna.

Caroline I'm afraid you can't right now.

Karlie I want to see her!

Caroline crosses to the door and knocks on the window.

Caroline (*to someone on the other side*) Can I –? Thanks.

Karlie Let me in there.

Caroline I can't.

A buzzer sounds and Caroline opens the door.

Karlie Let me in there! I'm her mother –

Karlie makes a grab for the door. Caroline steps in front of her. Karlie tries to push past her but Caroline won't have it.
She quickly jerks the clipboard up in front of Karlie's face and Karlie steps back, more surprised than anything.

What the –?

Caroline You sit down and you wait and I will tell you when you can see your daughter.

She goes, closing the door behind her.

Karlie You can't do that.

Yells.

You can't do that! You –! Oh my God!

She turns back into the room. Peter is still asleep. She rushes over, hits him with every word.

You are so fucking useless!

He turns over to avoid her, never opening his eyes.

Peter Stop it . . .

Karlie Peter?! Fuck! FUCK!

Stumped. Helpless. Then she picks up the phone, hits speed dial. Someone answers.

Mom?

End of scene.

SCENE TWO

The kitchen of a modest ranch house, four days later. The kitchen is dated but very clean. There is a table, covered with a floral table cloth, and surrounded by four chairs. This is the hub of the house. There is a pile of mail, and a large collection of vitamin and herbal medicine bottles. There is also a Glade candle, which is lit. Cindy, forty, and Caroline are in the kitchen. Cindy wears nursing scrubs with some sort of purple design on them, and white leather nursing shoes. Caroline is inspecting Cindy's kitchen. She has a clipboard with a form, which she makes notes on. On the table are her travel mug of coffee and her shoulder bag filled with files. Caroline is looking in the cabinet under the sink.

Cindy I'll get childproof latches for that one. And I'll move –

She goes to the cabinet and pulls out bottles of Soft Scrub, Windex, etc., and puts them on the counter top.

I'll move all this to where she can't reach it –

Caroline She's not even crawling yet.

Cindy But I want you to know that I know what to do. If I fail, you put Luna in foster care, right?

Caroline Right. But let's not get ahead of ourselves. Okay? You can leave the Windex under the sink for now.

Looks at the form.

So what are your hours? At St Luke's?

Cindy Seven to four. Or six to five, really, with traffic –

Caroline Have you thought about who would take care of Luna while you're at work?

Cindy My friend Allyssa runs a daycare out of her house –

Caroline Is she licensed?

Cindy Yes, ma'am. And she said, she can definitely take her.

Caroline hands her the form.

Caroline Would you write her name and address here for me?

Cindy Yes, ma'am.

Writes.

Caroline You don't have to call me 'ma'am'.

Cindy I'm sorry. I'm so nervous.

Holds the form out to Caroline, who looks at it.

Caroline I'll need a phone number, too.

Cindy Yes, ma'am.

Caroline (*smiles*) You really are nervous, aren't you?

Cindy I know I shouldn't be, but I keep –
I keep thinking what you must think of me. At St Luke's, we have the Child Protection Centre, where they bring in children who've been abused, for exams –

Caroline I'm familiar with the CPC –

Cindy Of course you are. I'm sorry –

Caroline No –

Cindy But that's it. I've seen them bring those kids in and I've seen the families. Sometimes the police will come in and arrest somebody right in the lobby. And I always judge them. I do. I think they're . . . failures. And now here I am, just like them –

Caroline You didn't do anything to Luna.

Cindy But if I'd seen Karlie and I didn't know who she was? Sitting there. I would have judged. I would have thought she was some dirty drug addict and that her mother didn't care. This is terrible of me but when she called, for a second I was so relieved she'd taken Luna to Mercy instead of St Luke's so nobody I worked with would know.

Caroline You know, there are two schools of thought on this. The first is that the apple doesn't fall far from the tree. The second is that – even the best of parents have kids who screw up. On their own.

Cindy I hope you went to the second school.

Caroline smiles.

Caroline Well. We'll see.

Looks at her form.

So I have a couple more things . . . Karlie and Peter's apartment? When was the last time you were there?

Cindy Two or three months ago?

Caroline What did you think of it?

Cindy It's not a nice apartment. They never bought any real furniture . . .

Caroline But it was clean?

Cindy Enough. I guess. Why? Was it –

Caroline It was bad.

Cindy It was?

18

Caroline Had you been busy? Is that why you hadn't been over?

Cindy She doesn't like me coming there.

Caroline Why not?

Cindy She thinks I judge her.
  Which I guess I do. I just did, didn't I? The way she looked . . . But what am I supposed to do? Just stand by while she does something stupid?

Caroline It's all right if you think smoking meth is stupid –

Cindy I didn't know they were smoking meth!

Caroline Okay –

Cindy If I'd known, I would have gone over there and taken Luna – just taken her –

Caroline Okay.

Cindy What possessed Karlie? To even think of that – ?

Caroline She said she needed it to stay awake at work. Because Luna was keeping her up at night.

Cindy She blamed the baby.

Caroline Everybody has their reasons.

Cindy She never takes responsibility.

  Beat. Caroline studies her.

Caroline Do you judge her, though? A lot?

Cindy I don't know. Do I?
  I think I'm helping. But then it always ends up in a fight.

Caroline What do you fight over?

Cindy Well.
  She wanted to buy one of those Maya wraps for Luna. And I told her, babies suffocate in those things.

Caroline Okay.

Beat.

Cindy And I think, she and Peter ought to get married. And I didn't jump up and down when she told me she was naming the baby 'Luna'. And I think Peter should get a job.

I have opinions and I say them. But they never listen.

Caroline I get it.

Cindy You have teenagers?

Caroline No, but I get it.

Caroline picks up a jar of nutritional supplement from the dining-room table.

Does this stuff work?

Cindy I take it for joint pain.

Caroline Huh.

The only other thing I need to ask you about is Karlie's record. It looks like she was arrested when she was fifteen?

Cindy How'd you know about that?

Caroline I pulled her record. It's sealed, though, because she was a juvenile, so I don't know what happened.

Do you want to tell me . . . ?

Cindy She was arrested for possession of marijuana. But the judge said if we did counselling her record would disappear. It would be expunged.

Caroline Did you do the counselling?

Cindy Yes.

Caroline Then somebody forgot to take care of it.

Cindy They said it would be like it disappeared.

Caroline It didn't.

Beat.

Cindy Karlie fell in with this crowd and they – the fun thing to do was get stoned and run around at the mall. I didn't even know any of it was going on until the police called me.

Caroline Why didn't you know?

Cindy I was working second shift, four to midnight.
    I'm not making excuses, but I had just gotten a divorce –

Caroline From Karlie's father?

Cindy Karlie's father died when she was three.

Caroline Oh. I'm sorry.

Cindy This other man I met at my church. We were married three years, but then . . .

Trails off.

Caroline But then?

Cindy He was being unfaithful to me. He left me.

Caroline That's tough. I'm sorry.

Cindy I had to go back to work, but all they could give me was second shift, so Karlie was home by herself after school.

Caroline (*overlapping on 'by'*) Home by herself.
    What kind of counselling did you get?

Cindy It was the counsellor at her school.

Caroline Did it do any good?

Cindy I thought it did. At first. She thought Karlie was bored in school, so they put her in this gifted and talented programme and that seemed to make her happy. But, then, that's where she met Peter. Was gifted and talented.

Caroline Really?

Cindy I didn't know it, but he was living by himself. His mother had gotten a new job down in Tennessee, at the Saturn factory. So she left him here, in an apartment. By himself. Karlie never told me that.

But it was a party house. And Karlie went there every night and she and Peter 'fell in love'. I guess. Or that's what she told me one night when she came home sloppy drunk. I said I didn't care if she was in love with him, if he was getting her drunk, then she couldn't see him any more, but she didn't care. She laughed at me and went right back to his apartment.

And this went on . . . for ever. It felt like. She wouldn't stop laughing at me. If I begged her, she laughed. If I tried to punish her, she laughed . . .

Caroline Okay. So what finally happened?

Cindy So finally I told her as long as she lived in my house she had to abide by my rules, and she said, 'Fine. I won't live in your house any more.' And she moved in with him. I called the police to see if she qualified as a runaway – to bring her home – but she was eighteen already and they said there was nothing they could do.

Beat.

I didn't know what to do.

Caroline I understand.

Indicating the refrigerator.

I'm going to open your refrigerator.

She does.

Cindy I haven't had any time to go shopping this week . . .

She takes a school picture off the refrigerator.

This is what she should look like. So you know. Her hair isn't really black.

Caroline studies the picture.

Caroline How old is she in this?

Cindy Twelve. When she was little, she was my best friend.

She puts the picture back on the refrigerator.

Caroline (*closing the refrigerator*) You do need to go shopping.

Cindy I know.

Caroline So this is what we call kinship care. It's somewhat different from foster care, in that you don't have to be licensed as a provider. But we try to give you the same services that a foster parent would have –

Cindy So I pass?

Caroline Yes, you pass.

Cindy Oh, thank God! I didn't know. I was so nervous.

To the ceiling. Joyful.

I'm sorry I doubted you! I'm sorry!

Small beat.

Caroline Okay. Now, you'll get the standard support payment –

Cindy (*confident now; her whole demeanour has changed*) Oh. I don't care about that.

Caroline You should, though. And next step is, we work up a case plan with Karlie and Peter –

Cindy What's a case plan?

Caroline Um, we spell out what they have to do in terms of rehab and counselling –

Cindy My pastor is wonderful. He was our associate pastor and when the last pastor retired, he was promoted.

Caroline Well. I'm glad to know that, I guess.

Cindy I mean, he can counsel Karlie. She has to go now. You're saying. Right?

Caroline Oh. Yes. But we have a . . . we contract with a counselling service for that. So we'll provide that.

Cindy I see.

Caroline But you should totally talk to your pastor. If that's helpful to you.

Cindy (*smiles*) I wouldn't be here without my faith. It was twelve years ago last month that I accepted Jesus as my personal saviour.

Caroline smiles.

Why are you smiling?

Caroline Was I smiling?

Cindy Is something funny?

Caroline No. I –

Thinks.

Whenever people say 'personal saviour' I always hear 'personal trainer' for some reason. I don't know why. And I don't know why that would be funny.

Indicates her coffee cup.

Way too much caffeine. What were you saying?

Cindy Nothing.

Caroline It's great that you have your faith to sustain you. That's important in difficult times.

Cindy Yes, it is.

Beat.

Caroline (*reaches in her bag*) I have a booklet that explains a lot about the kinship care . . .

She writes on the back of the booklet.

This is the number for my direct line, and my cell phone number. I'm all out of cards . . .

She hands the booklet to Cindy.

There'll be interim court dates to assess how Karlie and Peter are doing. The first one's in a month. At each stage we make a recommendation to the court depending on Karlie and Peter's progress. Have they made reasonable efforts?

Cindy Reasonable efforts?

Caroline Towards reunification. That's the goal.

Cindy Luna can stay with me for ever. As far as I'm concerned.

Caroline That's great. But reunification is always the goal.

Cindy Who makes the decision in the end? About whether or not they should have her back?

Caroline The judge makes the final decision.

Cindy But you're the one who knows what's going on . . .

Caroline Yes . . . ?

Cindy So he probably really relies on your recommendation.

Caroline Well . . . yeah.

Cindy That's an awesome responsibility.

Caroline It is.
So, I'll get started on the paperwork. Can you be at the hospital at four?

Cindy Of course.

Caroline Great. I'll give you a starter kit with diapers and dry formula. And you'll need a crib –

Cindy I still have Karlie's in the basement.

Caroline Right.

Cindy (*smiles*) I've done this before.

Caroline You have.
  Okay then. I look forward to working with you, Cindy –

Cindy You know, it may seem funny to you, but I think Jesus *is* a sort of personal trainer.

Caroline I shouldn't have said that. I'm really . . .

  Makes a crazy noise.

Whaaa!
  I have almost ninety cases right now. I'm always late for my next appointment.

Cindy But you're right. He's always asking us to be our best. To try harder. To keep going in spite of the pain. And there's been a lot of pain –

Caroline I'm sorry if I offended you.

Cindy No. I loved it.
  Because, Miss Cox? The thing with Jesus? Is He always gets results.

  End of scene.

SCENE THREE

Caroline's office, ten days later. The office is furnished with standard-issue everything. The only personal touch is a healthy potted ivy. There are stacks of files that

cannot fit into the filing cabinets. Organised chaos,
basically.

Karlie and Peter sit across from Caroline's desk. This
time it is Karlie who is in a funk, slumped down in
her chair. Peter is alert. Hyper-alert. Now he has the
jumpy leg.

Peter Do you want me to come and meet you and I can
ride the bus back with you?

Karlie No.

Peter Then what do you want?

She doesn't answer.

I can't read your mind. You have to tell me what you
want.

Karlie I want my own car.

Caroline starts to enter the office. They don't see her.
She stops and observes.

Peter Well, we don't have a car. So do you want me to
come and meet you?

She doesn't answer.

Do you want me to come and meet you?

Karlie I thought your dad was going to give us his truck.

Peter When he buys a new one. He doesn't have the
money yet.

Karlie He's totally playing you.

Peter Give him his props. He gave us a TV –

Karlie Used.

Peter He gave me fifty dollars last month. He gave us all
that cheese.

Karlie Used.

Peter smiles.

Peter Give him his props.

Karlie doesn't answer.

Give my pops his props.

Karlie Props to your pops.

Peter Mad props to my pops –

Caroline's heard enough.

Caroline Sorry to keep you waiting.

Karlie slips back into her funk. She stares at the floor throughout the following. But Peter sits up.

Peter That's okay.

Caroline How'd the visit go?

Peter It was great. Hard, but great.

Caroline She looks good, I think.

Peter She looks really terrific. We miss her. It's been, like, two weeks.

Small beat. Peter looks at Karlie, annoyed.

She was grabbing Karlie's finger. They have a connection –

Karlie She saw.

To Caroline, still not making eye contact.

You're watching us, right? Through that mirror?

Caroline Sometimes I am. Sometimes some of my colleagues are. Sometimes nobody is.

Karlie Right.

Caroline hands Peter a piece of paper.

Caroline So, we've got you set up with a woman named Gina Thorpe for counselling. For Mondays at the Behavioural Health Centre. Do you know where that is?

Peter We can find it.

Caroline You'll also, on Mondays, attend parenting classes. Then – the only glitch with your plan is Brill Street Centre is full up, in-patient and out-patient, so I had to put you on a waiting list for that. In the meantime, Karlie, I've got you placed with a group that meets at Hillcrest –

Peter What is Brill Street?

Caroline Rehab.

Peter Right. Okay. That's different from counselling?

Caroline It is. You have to do both. But there's no room in rehab. The best I can do right away is this support group. It meets on Tuesdays and Thursdays –

Peter What time?

Caroline Seven. Karlie? Does that work with your work schedule?

Peter It works.

Caroline Can Karlie answer me please?

Karlie Yes. Fine.

Caroline But that's only for mothers. It's called 'Mothers Off Meth'. Or MOM.

Karlie Clever.

Caroline Yes.
So, Peter, you'll have to join a men's group at Narcotics Anonymous that meets . . .

Consults more papers.

Also on Tuesdays and Thursdays but at the community centre.

Peter Just tell us where to be and we will be there.

He taps his fingers on the arm of the chair, super fast.
Caroline studies them for a moment.

Caroline What's going on here?

Peter What do you mean?

Caroline You gave a urine sample when you came in. What's it gonna tell me?

Peter It's negative. It's totally negative. It's totally, completely negative.

Caroline Uh-huh.

Peter The thing is this: have you ever done meth?

Caroline No.

Peter If you're not, you know, completely tweaked out? You're crashing, and so she's crashed and I'm trying to maintain an alternative mode of not crashing.

Caroline With?

Peter Amp.

Caroline Amp?

Peter High-energy drink. It's like Red Bull –

Caroline Oh.

Peter It's totally legal.

Caroline How many have you had?

Peter Today?

Caroline Yes.

Peter Six?

Caroline looks at her watch.

I know. It's bad, right?

Caroline You're going to give yourself a heart attack.

Peter I think it's a chance I have to take.

Caroline You really only started smoking a month ago?

  Peter nods.

Just, out of the blue?

Peter And meth is so yesterday, right?

Karlie All the cool kids are doing heroin.

Caroline Well, you're in pretty good shape, considering.

Peter We are?

Caroline You still have all your teeth.

  Handing them papers.

So here's the info for your meetings –

Karlie Ask about my mother.

Peter What? Now?

Karlie Ask.

Caroline What about her?

Peter I guess we didn't want to have – we were wondering – we understand about this whole process?

Caroline Yes?

Peter But – can Luna stay with somebody else?

Caroline Somebody else?

Peter Karlie and I really feel really strongly that we don't want Luna living with Karlie's mom.

Caroline Why?

  Peter looks to Karlie again. Karlie stares at the floor.

Peter She's like, doing some things we don't approve of. Karlie.

Caroline Like what?

Peter Karlie? Please talk to the lady.

Karlie What?

Peter Tell her what she did.

Caroline (*overlapping*) I've got, like, five minutes here.

Karlie (*looking at the front of the desk now*) She had her baptised against my explicit wishes not to have her baptised.

Caroline And?

Karlie Luna's not her daughter. She doesn't get to do that shit to her.

Peter It totally goes against our belief system.

Caroline Which is what?

Karlie Which is we don't have one so don't go putting the mark of Jesus on my daughter's forehead, thank you.

   Caroline sighs.

Caroline Look. Here's the deal. Your mom's a nurse –

Karlie Nurse's assistant.

   Small beat. Caroline didn't know this.

Caroline Well, maybe you don't share her belief system, but the only other option is I put Luna in foster care.

Karlie I would prefer that, please.

Caroline We're so overcrowded she'd be in a home with like, nine or ten other kids who may or may not be sociopaths. Through no fault of their own. Is that what you want?

Karlie Yes.

Peter No. We want her in a good home –

Karlie I don't want her with my mom!

Caroline Karlie, if you don't want your mother baptising Luna, your only real option is to get your shit together and get her back. Okay?

Caroline stands.
Karlie finally looks at her directly.

Karlie I'm not stupid.

Caroline I know you're not stupid. Neither one of you is, but –

Peter (*correcting her*) Are.

Caroline What?

Peter Neither one of us *are*.

Caroline Is.

Peter Really?

Caroline Yes.

Peter Huh.

Caroline But –

Peter It's singular?

Caroline Yes.

Peter So . . . even though the 'you' is plural –

Caroline 'Neither' is the subject and that's singular.

Peter (*likes learning new things*) Cool.

Beat.

Caroline I have no idea what I was saying.

Karlie You said, 'But –'

Caroline But. Also – you called your mom from the hospital so I thought you would want her to take Luna.

Peter You did what?

Karlie doesn't answer.

Why the fuck did you do that?

No answer.

Karlie!

Karlie I don't know.

Peter It's like you lived under Stalin or something.

To Caroline.

She totally has this learned helplessness.

To Karlie.

You totally identify with your oppressors.

Karlie I thought maybe she could be a character witness or something, I don't know.

Peter She hates you!

Karlie You were there! You could have stopped me. Dumb-ass.

Peter Sheep.

Beat.

Caroline If you're through –

Karlie (*to Peter*) I'm sorry. I didn't know what to do. I was so scared.

To Caroline.

We didn't know she was so sick. She never got sick like that before. We didn't know. It's not like we don't love her. We so totally love her –

Peter (*overlapping*) It's epic. Like when she's asleep and you look at her eyelids and her little eyes are moving under there and you want to know everything she's thinking, like you want to actually meld with her –

Karlie (*overlapping*) And you're like you fucking little fucking little perfect little fuck.

Beat.

Peter (*to Karlie*) We're idiots.

Karlie We are. But we're not mean or anything. We're not bad.

To Caroline.

We're stupid but we're not bad.

Pause.

Caroline I know you're not. Nobody is.

Peter Are.
I'm kidding.

Beat. Caroline might smile.

Caroline Nevertheless. Luna is with your mom until you can get her back.
I have to ask you guys to excuse me now. I have to be in court at two.

Peter I'm sorry we kept you.

He gets Karlie up and starts her out.

Let's go.

Caroline I'll see you next week.

Peter Wait – do we have another appointment?

Caroline I have to do another home inspection of your place. Before your court date. This one's a 'drop-in'.

Peter Okay.

Karlie Why is it called that?

Caroline I'm not sure when, but probably Friday.

Peter Okay.

Karlie Is it supposed to be a surprise?

Peter Thanks for talking to us and everything.

Karlie I'm confused.

Peter Shhh. It's okay.

To Caroline.

Goodbye.

Caroline Goodbye.

As they leave . . .

Karlie If it's a surprise, why did she tell us? Was she supposed to tell us that?

They're gone. Beat.

Caroline No.

End of scene.

SCENE FOUR

Two hours later. A table in the basement break room of the county courthouse. Caroline and Lourdes, eighteen, sit across from each other. Caroline has a vending-machine cup of coffee, Lourdes a can of Diet Coke.

Caroline How does it feel?

Lourdes Kinda weird. Emancipated.

Caroline You can just haul off and do anything now.

Lourdes I know.

Caroline I mean, within reason. Anything good. Anything fun, though, too. But not too fun.

36

Lourdes I know.

Caroline I'm sorry. I'm just . . . I want you to know that I think you can do anything you want.

Lourdes Thank you.

Caroline When do you move into your dorm?

Lourdes August 28th.

Caroline And you're okay with Mrs Del Rosario until then?

Lourdes She said it's no problem as long as I help out with the little kids.

Caroline What about breaks?

Lourdes She said Thanksgiving I could come back, but Christmas, she's going to Mindanao to see her family.

Caroline Maybe your room mate will invite you home or something . . .

Lourdes Maybe.

Caroline (*overlapping*) We'll see.
   So we should set up monthly aftercare meetings. But remember, I'm just your advocate now. I'm just here as a resource.

Lourdes Do you ever stop working?

Caroline What?

Lourdes You're always like . . .

Makes a serious face and pretends to write something.

On topic.

Caroline Yeah . . . I kinda . . . Maybe.

Lourdes You're not my caseworker any more. We should talk like . . . *friends.*

Caroline Really? Like . . . what should I say?

Lourdes Like what do you do for fun?

Caroline Oh. Well . . .

Pause.

I have a country house. It was my grandparents' house. Out in Tipton. They had a farm and I still own about ten acres. I still – on weekends – I like to go out and garden and bird-watch. There's a little stream. So migratory birds come through in the spring sometimes. Warblers.

Lourdes So you're like an old . . . weekend . . . retired lady.

Caroline laughs.

Caroline Five more years. And I can take early retirement. Not that I'm counting. Every single day.

They laugh. Beat.

So, we have presents . . .

Lourdes Seriously?

Caroline Yeah.

She reaches into her bag and pulls out a stuffed, white teddy bear holding a red-satin heart.

Here's your you've-aged-out-of-the-system-teddy-bear, complete with attached satin heart –

Lourdes It's not seriously called that, is it?

Caroline No. But we do give them to everybody.

Lourdes Even the guys?

Caroline Yeah. I did once, but . . .

Lourdes It didn't really go over?

Caroline No.

Cliff, thirty-five, enters. He is in between meetings, running late, but able to be in the moment as well.

Cliff Sorry I'm late!

Lourdes Hey, Mr Carlson.

Caroline Hi, Cliff.

Cliff Lourdes. Congratulations are in order! I want to –

Holds out his arms.

Can I give you a hug?

Lourdes Sure.

She stands and they hug.

Cliff (*to Caroline*) This is okay, right? Now that she's eighteen?

Caroline I don't know. That might make it not okay . . .

Cliff So everything went smoothly?

Caroline Smooth as silk.

Lourdes We got a standing ovation from the judge.

Cliff Did you?

Caroline (*to Lourdes*) That was a first for me. Just so you know.

Cliff (*to Lourdes*) Now when do you start school?

Lourdes Orientation week starts August 29th.

Cliff Terrific. You have to study hard, okay? There's nothing more important than education. Like me.

I went back to school for my Master's degree and that's what put me in line to head up our office. And some day I might even become a regional director if I work hard enough.

That's my dream. And you need to have a dream, too.

Lourdes Okay.

Cliff You know, community college is a great start, but if you can transfer to a four-year school, that's an even greater start.

Caroline How 'bout we take it one step at a time . . .

Lourdes (*to Cliff*) That's my goal.

Cliff Terrific.

   Small beat.

Caroline Do you know who your room mate is?

Lourdes Not yet. They have like a room-mate finder? I filled out the questionnaire but it hasn't matched me up with anybody yet.

Caroline My freshman year room mate never did her laundry. She soaked her dirty underwear in a bucket under her bed –

Lourdes Gross!

Caroline She forgot it once and it started to smell . . .

Cliff (*overlapping*) Why are you telling her this?

Caroline I don't know.

Cliff (*to Lourdes*) I'm sure your room mate will be very clean.

Lourdes I really want to find out who it is so I can see what all she's bringing . . .

Caroline Speaking of which –

   Hands her a greeting card.

– we also got you this.

Lourdes Thank you.

Caroline Open it. There's a gift card –

Lourdes pulls out a Target gift card.

Lourdes Thank you!

Caroline We figured you'd want to buy some neat stuff for your place –

Lourdes (*sees*) It's for two hundred dollars . . .!

Caroline We all chipped in.

Cliff gives her a questioning look.

Everybody signed the card.

Cliff What does it say?

Lourdes (*reads*) 'Congratulations, Lourdes. We're so proud of you.' 'Way to go, girl.' 'Good luck in college.' 'Good luck.' 'Good luck at Kirkwood.'
   "I'm honoured to know you.'

She looks at Caroline.

Caroline I am.

Lourdes Tell everybody thank you.

Cliff Hang on. I didn't get to sign it.

Caroline I'm sorry, Cliff –

Cliff I was probably out of the office. Hand it over.

Lourdes hands over the card. Cliff writes. Under this.

Caroline And what are your hours at the Quick Trip?

Lourdes They gave me almost forty till I leave.

Caroline So you'll be able to save up a little?

Lourdes (*nods*) I still want to buy a car.

Caroline Yeah. Think about that. You have to factor in insurance and gas, too –

Lourdes I know. But, I want to go to Chicago and see my sister –

Caroline Can she come here?

Lourdes I guess.

Caroline Maybe that would be better. If she came here first.

Lourdes nods, deflated. Small beat.

I'm not telling you what to do.
     You know your PAL stipend should kick in on the first –

Lourdes It's okay.

Cliff has finished.

Cliff Here.

Hands the card back to Lourdes.

Lourdes (*reads*) 'Lourdes. You are named for a place where miracles happen, but the real miracle is you.' Gosh.

Caroline Wow. Cliff.

Cliff See? I'm not a complete Neanderthal.

Beat. Lourdes is obviously touched.

Lourdes I'm going to put the card like this –

She tucks the card behind the heart on the bear.

– so it looks like he's holding the card, too.

Cliff Who gave you the bear?

Lourdes Caroline.

Caroline (*overlapping*) We all gave it to her. We have a whole –

Stops.

It's a tradition. For all our super great . . .

Searches. Gives up. Laughs.

I don't know what to call you. You're not a ward any more. You're not a client . . .

Cliff She's a miracle.

Beat.

Caroline I guess that's it. You're a miracle.

Quickly.

Who also worked really, really hard to get where you are. Let's not forget that. Okay?

Lourdes Okay.

Caroline Okay!

End of scene.

SCENE FIVE

Cindy's kitchen, the following night. There is now a stroller and car seat in the kitchen. Baby bottles are drying on a rack on the counter. A large can of dry formula is next to them.

Cindy and Pastor Jay sit at the kitchen table. Pastor Jay is in his late thirties. He is dressed casually in slacks and a polo shirt.

Cindy and the Pastor each have a cup of coffee in front of them. Pastor Jay is typing notes on a low-end laptop. He's showing Cindy what he's doing on the computer.

Pastor Jay This new programme divides the books up and categorises them by colour. So all the historical books are green, for example. So if you want to read the history, you just work your way through. Although, honestly, I'd skip Leviticus.

They laugh. He drinks his coffee.

What's this coffee?

Cindy Hazelnut.

Pastor Jay It's got an almost chocolate aftertaste –

The doorbell rings. Cindy gets up to answer and Pastor Jay stands.

Don't be nervous.

Cindy I'm not.

She exits. From off, we hear her open the door.

Miss Cox.

Caroline (*off*) I wish you'd call me Caroline.

Cindy (*off*) Thank you for coming over. I know it's past your work hours –

They enter the kitchen.

Caroline It was easier for me to do this than try to find time tomorrow . . .

Sees Pastor Jay.

Cindy This is Pastor Jay Lawrence, who I told you about.

Caroline Hello.

They shake.

Pastor Jay It's a pleasure to meet you, Miss Cox.

Caroline 'Caroline' is really okay.

Pastor Jay Caroline then. Would you like a cup of coffee? Cindy made some really terrific coffee.

Caroline No, thanks. If I drink it this late I can't sleep.

44

Pastor Jay Not a problem for me. I always sleep like a baby.

 Every night I wake up at three a.m. and start bawling.

They all laugh. Caroline's laugh ends soonest.

Caroline (*to Cindy*) So what was it you couldn't tell me over the phone?

Cindy Oh. Well . . .

Pastor Jay (*offering her a chair, which she is reluctant to take*) Why don't we all sit down? Could Cindy get you something else? Some herbal tea?

Caroline I'm really fine. Thank you. So what can I do for you?

Pastor Jay Down to business. I like that. Well, Caroline, we have a problem and we wondered if you could help us with it. We think you know that Cindy and Karlie have been fighting over this baptism thing –

Cindy I didn't baptise Luna.

Caroline Then it was a misunderstanding.

Cindy It was a blessing ceremony and I told her that and she acted like she didn't even know what that was –

Pastor Jay puts his hand on Cindy's arm.

Pastor Jay We should explain.

Cindy I'm sorry.

Pastor Jay It's all right.

To Caroline.

Caroline, in our church we believe you have to be at the age of accountability before you can be baptised. It's the fruition of a conscious choice. It marks the day you decide for Christ.

Cindy Karlie decided when she turned ten so she knows we didn't baptise Luna.

Pastor Jay But more to the point, Karlie said some really unfortunate things to her mom on the phone.

Cindy She called me a 'bitch'.

Caroline That is unfortunate.

Pastor Jay And then she threatened to kidnap Luna.

Caroline What?

Cindy She said that if I didn't stop taking her to church that she was going to come over here and take her and run away to Mexico.

Caroline Well, that's no good, but I doubt she meant it.

Pastor Jay Miss Cox, how well do you know Karlie?

Caroline Not well.

Pastor Jay I do know Karlie well. And I love Karlie, I do. But she is not a stable young lady.

Caroline But isn't this just how she talks when she's mad? Isn't she just kind of . . . nineteen? I mean, she doesn't even have a car.

Cindy So you don't take this threat seriously?

Caroline I do. Insofar as, yes, unacceptable behaviour. But insofar as actual threat? I guess I don't.
    And, all I can really do right now, at . . . eight-twenty on a Thursday is wait and talk to her tomorrow –

Getting up.

Which I will absolutely do –

During this, Cindy looks to Pastor Jay. He gives her a go-ahead nod.

Cindy Then, Miss Cox, I want to inform you that I want full custody of Luna. I want to adopt her as soon as possible.

Caroline What the ffff . . . heck?

Beat. Caroline sits.

Wow. You want to adopt her?

Cindy Yes.

Caroline Do you know what that means?

Pastor Jay It means that Cindy would be able to raise Luna and love her as her own. Right?

Caroline But, for you to adopt, you have to petition for termination of both Karlie and Peter's parental rights. Which . . . I don't think you really want to do that.
  What you really want to do, I think, is petition for a temporary guardianship –

Cindy But that doesn't give me any rights.

Caroline It gives you certain rights.

Pastor Jay But not if the state rules for reunification.

Caroline That's . . . true. How do you know that?

Cindy Our attorney told us.

Caroline You have an attorney?

Pastor Jay One of my parishioners who's offered to help us –

Cindy He said TPR is the only way to go if I want this to be permanent.

Caroline You're using the acronyms now, huh?

Cindy It's how he says it.

Caroline Right. Well, he also should have told you that it's only been a couple of weeks since we placed Luna with you, and no judge is going to terminate parental rights so soon.

Pastor Jay But he says there's this thing called 'concurrent planning.'

Looks at notes on his computer.

That while Karlie and Peter are working on their case plan, you can also work with us *concurrently* on a case plan for adoption. That this would not be considered 'inconsistent' because the goals reflect 'divergent possible outcomes'.

Caroline Wow.

Pastor Jay (*to Cindy*) She said 'wow' again –

Caroline You've done your research.

To Cindy.

Here's the thing. We can do that. We often do that. But with kinship care, I only recommend it as a last resort. And most grandparents never want to do that.

Pastor Jay Why not?

Caroline Because they want their children to get better. Karlie is in the very beginning stages of her recovery. If Cindy files for TPR, she's saying to Karlie –

To Cindy.

– that you don't think she even stands a chance. That you don't trust her or have any faith in her.

Cindy I don't.

Caroline But she's your daughter.

Cindy But I don't have faith in Karlie or you or me or anybody, because I don't have faith in any one person. You can't put your faith in people.

Pastor Jay Cindy doesn't indulge in situational thinking.

Caroline I don't know what that means.

Cindy This world is not real. This world is a vapour.

Caroline waits for more.

Pastor Jay What Cindy is saying is that the only thing that's real, ultimately, is the heavenly kingdom of Jesus.

Cindy But Luna can't get there unless she's saved. And if she grows up with Karlie, she'll never be saved –

Pastor Jay Like I've said, we've been dealing with Karlie's rebellion for years now and we've seen this pattern. She shapes up, for a little while, but then she always relapses –

Cindy She can't resist temptation. She falls back into sin and she deliberately chooses the unrighteous path. And she'll take Luna down that same path and if Luna doesn't know the righteous path then I've condemned her –

Towards Luna's room.

I've lost her, too –

Pastor Jay It's all right.

Cindy The end days are upon us –

Caroline The end days?

Cindy The signs are here. The wars in the Middle East. All the floods and earthquakes, the abortions –

Pastor Jay is watching Caroline. He stops Cindy, again, with a hand on her arm.

Pastor Jay It's all right, Cindy. Let's back up –

Cindy But –

Pastor Jay Cindy, what we want to focus on here is that concurrent permanency plan. What we want to hear is whether Caroline is going to support us in that or not.

   Beat.

Caroline Okay. Well I don't know what to tell you. I mean, the only kind of thinking I can do, is situational thinking. Because I have to place children. In the here and now.

Pastor Jay And here we are talking about vapours and eternal kingdoms when all you're thinking is, 'What do I tell the judge?' Am I right?

Caroline Yes.

Pastor Jay Then let me speak objectively here. You've got two unemployed drug addicts who almost killed their baby through neglect –

Caroline Karlie still has her job at Perkins –

Pastor Jay (*overlapping*) And here –

   Points offstage.

Go look at Luna's room. See what Cindy can give that child. See the clothes Cindy has bought for her, and the toys. The changing table, the rocking chair. Look at Luna's colour. Weigh her. See how good she looks. That's what Cindy's done. Not the church. Not God.

   Go see what Cindy has provided. And then tell me, honestly, Caroline: where do you think Luna belongs?

   End of scene.

Caroline's office, the following Friday. Caroline is on her computer. Cliff enters.

Cliff You had some cases for me to sign off on?

Caroline Yeah. For Monday . . .

She looks for two files in the stack on her desk. Finds one, hands it to Cliff.

That's the Campbell case. I'm asking for a three-month continuance.

Cliff What's the boyfriend situation?

Caroline He was remanded back to jail.

Cliff reads for a second. Closes the file.

Cliff Excellent. A three-month continuance seems right on. And just please note that on the spreadsheet on the server.

Caroline Will do.

He wishes she would do it now. As Caroline finds the second file.

Cliff Hey! What was the deal on that Target gift card?

Caroline What Target gift card?

Cliff takes out his wallet.

Cliff For Lourdes. I didn't get to contribute. How much do I owe you?

Caroline Oh. Nothing. Don't worry about it.

Cliff I know I haven't known her for as long as you guys . . .

Caroline Nobody gave me anything. I bought it myself. So don't worry about it.

Cliff You shouldn't do that.

Caroline But she's going to show up at her dorm room and her room mate's going to have a ton of stuff. And Lourdes is going to have, like, one suitcase and a former foster mom.

Cliff It's not the thought, it's the fact that you bought it yourself. It's actually a policy. You shouldn't do that.

Small beat.

Caroline Her case was closed, though. So it was a gift from me, a private citizen, to a fully emancipated adult. Policy doesn't apply.

Small beat.

Cliff Okay! Fair enough.

Caroline (*holds out the file*) The next one I'm asking for three months, too. The baby is six months old. Parents are meeting plan –

Cliff (*takes the file but doesn't open it*) The little bear was cute. Who got her the bear?

Caroline We have a whole case of them in the storeroom. Mimi bought them . . . years ago. She thought it'd be cute to give them out whenever the kids turned eighteen.

Cliff Mimi, huh?

Caroline Yeah.

Beat. Cliff opens the file, reads.

Cliff Minor Child: Luna Gale.
   Weird name. Is she a vampire baby?

Caroline No.

Cliff It sounds like it's from one of those books. With the sexy vampires.

Caroline Yeah. Anyway, baby's in kinship care now, so no rush I don't think.

Standard three-month continuance. Is what I'm requesting.

Cliff (*studies the file*) The grandmother's requested a concurrent permanency plan.

Caroline She has.

Cliff You want to get that started?

Caroline I feel like it's premature.

Cliff But it's an open safety.

Caroline But she's only had the baby a few weeks.

Cliff What's the harm, though?

Caroline The grandmother's instigating it with an eye toward TPR.

Cliff waits.

The mother is in early stages of recovery and I feel like this might set her back.

Cliff waits.

If she feels like her own mother thinks she's a lost cause?

Cliff Is she a lost cause?

Caroline I don't think so. I think she's messed up. I think she and the dad are both basically messed up but they also seem like they love each other and they want to do right by their daughter. My gut feeling is that they're . . . sweet.

Cliff (*looks at the file*) Condition of parents' home was deplorable . . .

Caroline That was my first visit, right after we took the baby.

Cliff (*reads*) 'Dirty dishes piled up in the sink. Several dead cockroaches, also in the sink.'

Beat. He looks at her.

Caroline They drowned.

Cliff (*reads*) 'Refrigerator and cabinets empty except for a box of Nutty Buddies, half a doughnut and a bag of marshmallows . . .'

Caroline There was also formula, and some PediaCare –

Cliff (*reads*) 'Fetid diapers and rotten food in garbage pail . . . Bedroom floor obscured by clothes and garbage.'

Small beat. To himself.

'Fetid.'

Caroline It means stinky.

Cliff I know. Were there drugs on the premises?

Caroline They weren't actually smoking in the apartment.

Cliff They claim.

Caroline Hair and blood on the baby tested negative on exposure.

Cliff Where were they using?

Caroline The mother at her workplace, apparently. And the father says he stepped outside on to the balcony.

Cliff The unemployed father.

Caroline He's a stay-at-home dad.

Cliff gives her a look.

It shows some basic level of concern –

Cliff Stepping outside to smoke meth?

Caroline As opposed to cooking it on an open hot plate with your toddler three feet away and a loaded revolver on the coffee table.

Which I've seen.

It does.

Cliff How does the place look now?

Caroline I haven't been back. I'm going tonight.

Cliff You're cutting it close, aren't you? Court date's Monday?

Caroline Do you want to lighten my caseload?

Cliff You know I can't.

Caroline Then get off my back.

Beat.

Cliff Recommend the concurrent permanency plan.

Caroline It's only been a month.

Cliff It's a contingency plan. That's all it is. And if the parents don't get their act together – which they won't – they're meth addicts – then when their six months is up –

Caroline (*overlapping*) They get a year –

Cliff The grandmother's there with open arms ready to adopt. That is streamlined. That is efficient. That is the way we should work.

He holds out the file, she doesn't take it.

What?

Caroline I think I may have made a mistake with the grandmother. I think she might be crazy.

Cliff Crazy how?

Caroline She thinks the world is coming to an end.

55

Cliff Like . . . how?

Caroline Like the end days. So she wants to adopt the granddaughter so she can make sure she's saved before the rapture comes.

Beat.

Cliff So she's a Christian.

Caroline She's a crazy Christian.

Cliff She's an Evangelical Christian.

Caroline She thinks the world is a vapour.

Cliff Is she smoking meth?

Caroline No.

Cliff Recommend the plan.

He holds out the file. Caroline doesn't take it.

Caroline Why can't she just wait and file for TPR when the year is out? No harm done.

Cliff Except we're involved for another six months with the expense and the oversight that entails –

Caroline Spoken like a true bureaucrat.

Cliff I have a budget I have to make work. But mostly, I don't think we should let these things drag on for ever based on some . . . gut feeling you have that they're 'sweet'.

Caroline My gut feelings are based on twenty-five years of experience –

Cliff I know.

Caroline I might have some idea what I'm doing. Okay?

Beat.

Cliff Look, I know, by all rights, you should have my job –

Caroline I didn't want your job. I just think it's ridiculous that I have to get your approval on every little decision I make when I was running my own cases for twenty-five years.

Cliff Well, this is what happens when an office loses children.

Indicates himself.

You get state-appointed oversight. I don't enjoy it any more than you do.

Caroline This office didn't lose any children. Mimi did. And now I'm being punished for something I never even knew was happening.

Cliff But you're level five. It's part of your job description to know what's happening.

Caroline But Mimi was the boss. She ran the briefings. If she didn't bring up a case, we didn't know it existed.

Cliff But there must have been a point when the kids were in the system –

Caroline What 'system'? We didn't have the spreadsheet on the server thing –

Cliff That I set up in an hour?

Caroline I'm explaining how it happened. Under Mimi, there was no system.

Cliff doesn't respond.

What?

Cliff I still think someone should've known. Is all.

Caroline By 'someone' you mean me.

Cliff She threw files away – she threw whole cases away –

Caroline She was overwhelmed.

Cliff Children disappeared and nobody noticed.

Caroline Do you think I haven't tried to find them? I'm the one who went through her office, I'm the one who –

Stops.

Found her fucking –

Stops.

Cliff You found her body. I know.

Caroline Then I went through her office. Her house. Her car. The woman kept case notes on Burger King wrappers. She wrote her suicide note on the back of her water bill. There weren't any files, there was shit. Piled everywhere. Like those goddamn teddy bears –

Gestures off.

She came in here with a case of teddy bears one day, all excited, like this would save the children. She was an idiot.

And she never talked about her cases with me because I never talked about mine with her. Nobody did. We just tried to ignore her and do our own work because she was a stupid, fat, idiot who couldn't keep up!

Cliff And you knew she was in trouble. And you didn't step in. That's my point.

Beat.

'Assists supervisor in monitoring case actions.' It's in your job description. You don't follow it whenever it suits you. You follow it all the time.

Caroline (*steady*) I have never lost a child.

Cliff High standard, there.

Caroline Oh – fuck you!

Pause.

Cliff You know, I don't appreciate the language. It's offensive. Don't use it any more.

He holds out the file.

What are you going to do? With this? On Monday?

Beat.

What are you doing to do –?

Caroline snatches the file back.

Caroline Recommend the goddamn concurrency plan!

Cliff Great, Caroline! That sounds right on!

End of scene.

SCENE SEVEN

Karlie and Peter's apartment, later that evening. Kitchen/ living-room combo. It is exactly the sort of apartment one would expect from two nineteen-year-olds. The couch was salvaged from the trash. An old piano bench serves as a coffee table. A TV sits on a stand of milk crates and an older-model video game console sits on the floor.

An umbrella stroller with a stuffed rabbit in it is against one wall. Other baby things are scattered about.

Peter, Karlie and Caroline are all standing. Peter wears cheap plastic yellow coverall bottoms (from Wal-Mart) over a dirty white T-shirt. Karlie wears a waitress uniform from Perkins: blue slacks and a khaki top with the Perkins logo (not cute). Peter holds a plate of home-made cookies. Caroline takes one.

Karlie We made them on Tuesday in case you came over on Tuesday because we didn't understand the whole 'surprise-that's-not-a-surprise' thing.

Caroline I was just trying to give you a heads-up.

Karlie But you said, 'probably Friday.' We started thinking it was some sort of test.

Peter We totally obsessed over it.

Karlie You don't really seem like somebody who would actually help us cheat.

Beat.

Peter Do you want some coffee? I can make some coffee.

Caroline No, thank you.

They wait for her to take a bite. She does.

It's good.

Karlie It's dry.

Caroline It's not. It's really good. Thank you. For this. That was . . . You baked.

Karlie I wanted to.

Beat.

Peter got a job. He's detassling.

Peter Thus the killer threads.

Karlie That's why the Band-Aids are back on his fingers. Because the corn tears up your fingers. Not because we're smoking again. In case you wondered.

Caroline How long does detassling last? Three weeks?

Peter Yeah.

Caroline You need to find something permanent.

Peter I know. I'm looking.

Karlie He has an interview at Auto Zone on Wednesday.

Caroline Auto Zone.
Did you guys ever think of going to college?

They laugh.

What?

Peter Who's going to pay for it?

Karlie (*overlapping*) I can't get in anywhere.

Caroline There are ways to pay for it. You get in-state tuition and –

To Karlie.

Weren't you both in the gifted and talented programme?

They laugh.

Karlie 'Gifted and talented' at our school meant instead of taking flower arranging twice, you took flower arranging once, and shop.

Caroline You're both smart, though. Right?

They both shrug.

Karlie My mom didn't think so. She wanted me to go to this unaccredited Christian school that my fucking freak of a stepfather picked out. It was in the basement of some church. Pathways Christian Academy –

Caroline (*overlapping*) Pathways Christian? Really?

Karlie So I could be illiterate. Yes.
But then I got arrested for smoking weed in the bathroom of the Chik-Fil-A and they wouldn't take me. High-five!

She holds out her hand for a high-five from Peter. He doesn't give it to her.

Peter Yeah. So. We were wondering, about our case plan? It's not that we're not doing great, because we are. But is there not something at rehab yet?

Caroline There's almost two hundred people on their waiting list.

Peter Oh. You didn't tell us that.

Caroline I didn't want you to think . . .

Peter That we wouldn't get in?

Caroline What about the support groups? Are those not helping?

Karlie They're helping tons.

Peter Come on. I'm trying to get us help here –

Karlie (*under her breath*) She's not the person to ask.

Caroline I am the person to ask.

Karlie But you're the one who judges us.

Caroline And finds you help. Which you have to, then, take. As I prescribe it.

They look at her.

So what's the problem with the groups?

Peter Well, my group never talks about drugs.

Caroline They don't?

Peter They're all, like, forty? And all they do is chain-smoke and complain about their bitch of an ex-wife or the bitch at the unemployment office. It oughta be called Misogynists Anonymous.

Caroline Okay. And what about Mothers Off Meth?

Karlie You mean MOM? It's, like, really helpful and supportive.

Peter Karlie –

Karlie I'm saying.

It's like, really helpful and supportive. And every night is a different night!

Tuesday was movie night. Thursday was craft night. We're learning how to crochet.

Caroline Craft night.

Peter Yeah.

Karlie Yeah.

Pause. Caroline seems really tired all of a sudden. Like all the exhaustion of the past however-many years has hit her at once. But she rallies.

Caroline And what about counselling?

Karlie Gina's okay. I like that she's so young.

Caroline Uh-huh.

Peter But she cancelled our next appointment.

Caroline I got her email. I'm sorry about that. We used to have more people . . .

She trails off.

They consolidated two offices – DHS offices? That's why we're Linn-Benton now –

Stops.

And then budget cuts and they laid off half the staff. But we still have two counties to cover. With half the staff. And we had some issues in our office that I . . . should have been more on top of . . .

So this is not an excuse or anything, I just want you to know that it's not that I don't want you to get help, because I do, it's just that there's not any help out there.

But as soon as there is, I'll get you some.

Karlie We weren't – you know – blaming.

Pause. Caroline can't quite rally again.

Peter We painted Luna's room. You should see it. Karlie painted stars on the ceiling.

Caroline doesn't respond.

With glow-in-the-dark paint.

Caroline doesn't respond.

Are you okay?

Caroline (*to Karlie*) Your mom wants to keep her.

Karlie What?

Caroline Your mom is filing for the termination of yours and Peter's parental rights and she wants permanent custody of Luna –

Karlie (*overlapping on 'custody'; pacing*) Oh no. No no no no no no.

The following all overlaps.

Peter She can do that?

Caroline She can do that, yes.

Peter Then what are we doing this for?

Karlie (*overlapping. To Peter*) I told you! From the second I told her she was like – you're not gonna be able to take care of this baby –

Caroline This isn't a done deal –

Peter So you can stop her?

Karlie Nobody can stop her! My whole life! My whole life! She gets everybody on her side – she makes everybody think I'm dirt –

Caroline Karlie, calm down –

Karlie She's going to make Luna hate me! Peter?!

Peter No she won't –

Karlie She's gonna make her be me!

Goes to kitchen.

I'm drinking vodka. I want some fucking vodka –

Caroline No you don't –

Peter (*overlapping*) We don't have any.

Karlie Nobody cares what you do. Even if you do it right.

She picks up her phone.

I'm calling the police –

Caroline No –

Karlie She kidnapped her!

Peter (*going for her phone*) Give it –

Karlie She wasn't supposed to keep her!

Caroline (*overlapping*) Calm down –

Peter Calm down.

Karlie Stop saying calm down to me!

Caroline You don't need to prove how upset you are. We get it –

Peter We totally get it –

Caroline Let's just dispense with the hysteria and just –

Motions to Karlie to sit.

Talk about what we're going to do.

Karlie doesn't move.

Come up with a strategy. Make a plan.

Peter Listen to the lady who's telling us the thing –

Karlie Why should I listen to her?!

Caroline Because I want to help you!

Peter (*overlapping*) For Luna!

Caroline We have to make sure Luna's –

Karlie Not completely fucked like I was?

Grabs her house keys.

I'm getting her back!

Heads for the door.

Peter (*steps in her path*) Stop it!

Karlie (*turns and takes another route*) I'll take her! She's mine! I can take her!

Caroline (*overlapping*) No –

She grabs Karlie by the arm.

You can stop this right now. This is what's going to sink you, right here. Do you understand me? Stop it!

Karlie I can't help it!

Caroline I know!

Karlie starts to cry. Caroline is nonplussed.

Oh God. Peter?

Caroline steps aside. Peter goes to Karlie to comfort her. But as soon as he touches her she jerks away.

Karlie Don't –

Peter (*used to this*) Okay –

Karlie Don't touch me!

Peter Fine!

They stand apart from each other, hurt. Caroline watches them.

Caroline (*to herself*) It's not like I don't know what I'm doing.

Peter What?

Caroline How were you fucked?

Karlie What?

Caroline You said you didn't want her to get fucked, like you. How were you fucked?

Karlie Entirely?
  What are you –

Caroline And your stepfather picked out the school? Pathways Christian?

Karlie So?

Caroline He was around.

Caroline thinks.

Karlie (*to Peter*) What is happening?

Peter I have no idea.

Caroline (*sharp*) Let me think this through, please.

She thinks for as long as it takes.

Okay.

To Karlie.

Sit down.

Karlie doesn't move.

Please sit down.

Karlie sits.

Okay. Let's back up. What happened to you when you were fifteen?

Karlie stares at her, confused.

Karlie When I was . . . ?

Caroline You smoked pot. Right? You started acting out? Your mom says it was her divorce but is that really what started it? Is that really why you started acting out? Because if there was something else, you should tell me.

Karlie Like what?

Caroline Like, maybe something your mom did or didn't do . . . or something your *stepdad* did . . . to you . . .

Karlie You mean like . . .
    Oh, no. He never . . .
    That never happened.

Caroline nods.

Caroline But what if it did.

Karlie But it didn't.

Caroline Karlie. Stay with me. What if it did?

End of Act One.

Act Two

One month later. The basement break room of the county courthouse. Lourdes and Caroline are having coffee. Lourdes looks different. She wears more revealing clothes, has a harder edge. She also has a tattoo of a blue fish under one collarbone that is only half hidden by her blouse. Lourdes' phone is on the table, face up.

Lourdes It's the whole seventh floor of Macy's and there's all these different choices, like noodles and Mexican and salads. It's mad expensive but my sister gets a employee discount so she bought me lunch. Then I went shopping for the rest of her shift but I couldn't afford anything there so I went over to this store called H and M and they had super cute stuff for way cheaper. That's where I got this sweater.

Caroline It's really cute.

Lourdes It was only like sixteen dollars.

Caroline I'm glad you had fun.

Lourdes I totally did.

Caroline How are classes?

Lourdes Good.

Beat. Lourdes checks her phone.

Caroline Sorry we had to meet here. I'm in court all day today.

Lourdes I don't care.

Beat.

Caroline I see you got a tattoo.

Lourdes I was wondering when you were going to say something.

Caroline Well. It's not . . . super visible and I didn't want you to think I was staring at your boobs.

Lourdes My sister and her boyfriend have tats, like, everywhere, and we went to their guy.

Caroline Did it hurt?

Lourdes Yeah. It still itches.

Caroline Is it infected?

Lourdes It's just red around the edges still, but it's fading.

Caroline Why a fish?

Lourdes It's a symbol of good luck in Chinese.

Caroline I didn't know that. Maybe I should get one.

Lourdes You're too old.

Caroline Oh my God. Thanks a lot.

Small beat.

Lourdes It was weird to see my sister.

Caroline Weird how?

Lourdes Like, all these little things I do that she does too? Like she's always popping her knuckles like me. And Alex said when we were in the next room he couldn't even tell which one of us was talking, we sound so much alike. Even though – we haven't seen each other in seven years.

Caroline Has it been that long?

Lourdes Marta said that's how strong blood is.
    She said she remembers you.

Caroline She does?

Lourdes She said that group home you put her in sucked.

Caroline Yeah, it probably did.

Lourdes Why'd you do that?

Caroline I didn't have a choice. You were easy to place because you were little. But there weren't any foster parents who would take Marta because they were scared, because of her record. It wasn't her fault, but there was no place else to put her.

Lourdes She said that home was sick.

Caroline Good sick or bad sick?

Lourdes Both sick. She said you could score anything there and people were fucking each other in the closets and shit –

Caroline Great.

Lourdes She told me all the drugs she did, it was like . . .

Counts off on her fingers to eight.

Caroline Great. What about now, is she still doing stuff?

Lourdes (*shrugs*) She likes to have fun.

Caroline But you're not into that.

Lourdes (*flat*) No. I don't like to have fun.

Beat.

We were wondering if you know where our mom is.

Caroline No.

Lourdes We both think she's probably dead.

Caroline I hope not.

Lourdes We think she died on the street.
Marta says she was schizophrenic.

Caroline She was definitely self-medicating for something.

Lourdes Marta said it'd be good to know if she was schizophrenic 'cause then we would know if we're going to get it.

Caroline What?

Lourdes She said if it was schizophrenia then there's a chance we'll get it too, like when we're thirty or twenty-eight or something. Right?

Beat.

Caroline There's an increased likelihood. I don't know what the percentages are. But there are much better drugs now than there used to be. Even if you get it, you don't have to end up like your mom. Okay?

Lourdes How do you know if you have it?

Caroline I don't know.

Lourdes Do you start hearing voices?

Caroline Some people start hearing voices. Are you hearing voices?

Lourdes No.

Caroline Are you feeling okay?

Lourdes I'm totally fine.

Caroline When are your mid-terms?

Lourdes Next week.

Caroline Do you feel prepared, or . . . ? I can't tell how you're feeling about school.

Lourdes It's fine.

Caroline That's so not an answer.

Lourdes It's fine. I'm doing fine.

She checks her phone.

Caroline You know, my mom was an alcoholic.

Lourdes You told me that already.

Caroline I know. But I think I told you in the context of, I know what it is to not have a mom who's around for you, right?

Lourdes At least you knew when she died.

Caroline Yeah. But the thing is, if you have a parent who's an alcoholic, you have a much higher risk of becoming an alcoholic, too. So I think I know the fear you're feeling about maybe ending up like your mom, too.

Lourdes You have control over that, though.

Caroline Not so much. I mean, you do, but you have to be vigilant. Like I have a friend who's never even touched alcohol because he doesn't want to end up like his dad.

Lourdes Do you drink?

Caroline I do socially. But I have sometimes worried I was drinking too much. And sometimes, I've been in places where I was maybe drinking wine at night by myself –

Lourdes You don't have a husband, right?

Caroline I'm divorced. But what I'm saying is, when I've been depressed or anxious or something, there have been times in my life when I've had a drink or something by myself.
   Even now, sometimes, I'm driving home at night and I pass by a bar and I think, Why not just go in and drink myself into a stupor?

Lourdes Why don't you?

73

Caroline Because! You can't just punt. That's my point. You have to . . . go to school and learn things and get smarter and . . . get a tattoo of a fish that says you're lucky. Some day you're going to have a nice house, and a family. Or a really great career and a dog. I don't know.

Lourdes I don't like dogs.

Caroline A cat, then. Just don't sell yourself short or close off options because you think maybe someday something bad might possibly happen. Okay?

Lourdes 'Cause if I work hard enough, I can totally have that cat or whatever?

Caroline Whatever you want. It doesn't have to be a cat –

Lourdes checks her phone.

Are you expecting a call?

Lourdes Just checking the clock. I have to go.

Caroline (*checks her watch*) I do too.

Lourdes stands.

Are you sure you're feeling okay?

Lourdes Totally. But I have to get to class.

Caroline What class?

Lourdes (*quickly*) Econ. It's my favourite class. The professor's really funny. I really feel like I'm learning a lot.

Caroline Okay.

Lourdes I hope you don't go in some bar and get drunk –

Caroline I'm not! That was my point.

Lourdes I'm just kidding.

They both start to go in different directions.

74

Caroline See you next month.

Lourdes Look, I don't know if I can make it next month, and it's not like – I don't have to be here, right?

Caroline Next month?

Lourdes Or ever. Like I don't lose my PAL stipend or anything do I? If we stop meeting?

Caroline It's never been required . . . to meet with me . . .

Lourdes I know.

Caroline But most people stick with Aftercare for at least a couple of years. We don't have to always meet in person. We can do it over the phone –

Lourdes Then maybe what if I just call you?

Caroline When?

Lourdes I don't know.

Lourdes starts to go.

Caroline Next week?

Lourdes Sure.

Caroline (*starts out*) Make me your ICE.

Lourdes What?

Caroline In Case of Emergency. On your phone, under contacts. Just make me your ICE.

Lourdes Why?

Caroline Do you have anybody? There?

Lourdes No. But – are you just assuming I'm going to have an emergency?

Caroline Just in case. Is all.

Beat.

Please?

Lourdes (*taking out her phone*) Fine. If it makes you feel better.

Caroline It does.

End of scene.

Caroline's office, one week later. Caroline is speaking to Cindy.

Cindy This is crazy! She's lying!

Caroline So you maintain that it never happened.

Cindy Yes!

Caroline And this is how you responded at the time.

Cindy To what? When?

Caroline She said she tried to tell you and you were in complete denial, you wouldn't acknowledge or listen, that it was like you didn't even hear her.

Cindy Because she never said anything because it never happened!

Caroline Okay. Let's just step back for a second and take a breath, okay? First of all, I'm not accusing you of anything. I just have to take this seriously –

Cindy Why?!

Caroline Because it's a hugely serious thing. As an allegation –

Cindy (*overlapping*) This is unbelievable. She knows that judge wants to give me Luna so she's told you this stupid lie and you're just buying right into it.

Caroline She didn't tell me. She told her counsellor. Her counsellor told me.

Cindy Then she's working the system.

Caroline I'm not naive, okay? But honestly, it explains a lot –

Cindy Please!

Caroline The sudden acting out at fifteen. The depression, the substance abuse, the early pregnancy. It's kind of textbook and just –

Cindy (*on 'book'*) It's crap!

Caroline Cindy.

Cindy It is! It's crap!

Caroline Don't interrupt me again. Please.

Beat.

Just because you don't believe it doesn't mean it didn't happen. And if it did happen and you refused to believe her then you put Karlie in physical and emotional jeopardy and that's a factor now in your petition for TPR and adoption.

Cindy What?

Caroline Because you want to adopt Luna I have to fully investigate this. And I have to draw up a case plan for you. I'm going to set you up with a counsellor at the Behavioural Health Centre –

Cindy This is a nightmare.

Caroline Then we'll determine if you should be allowed to continue as Luna's caretaker.

Cindy But I'm adopting her.

Caroline (*sighs*) Cindy, if you looked the other way while your husband was abusing Karlie, and you refuse to address that, then the department's position is that you cannot have custody of Luna.

Small beat.

I don't know how much clearer I can make this . . .

Cindy So I have to – I have to go to this counsellor and say that this thing happened that never happened and if I don't say it happened, you can take Luna away from me?

Caroline You don't have to say anything.
You just have to admit that it might have happened, and Karlie might be telling the truth.

Cindy I have to lie.

Caroline No –

Cindy The government is going to make me lie.

Caroline We just want you to consider that it might have happened. That maybe Karlie wasn't possessed by the devil so much as she was molested by her stepfather.

Beat.

Cindy You're enjoying this.

Caroline I'm not enjoying this.

Cindy You are. You're enjoying it.

Caroline What could possibly be enjoyable about this?

Cindy Because you're an anti-Christian bigot.

Caroline That is so not true.

Cindy But I won't meet your hate with hate. I'll meet it with love.
Because that's what God counsels: patience and understanding.

End of scene.

*The Perkins where Karlie works, that night. Karlie, Peter
and Caroline sit at a table. They are all drinking coffee.
There is a carafe of coffee on the table and a piece of pie
in front of Caroline, which she doesn't touch.*

*Karlie is in her uniform, but she looks more 'normal.'
She has forgone the goth eye make-up and is not wearing
black fingernail polish any more. Peter wears khakis and
an Auto Zone polo shirt.*

*They talk in a weirdly self-conscious way. Like they're
afraid they're being bugged and want to make sure
everything is said correctly, for the record.*

Caroline (*to Karlie*) You never told the counsellor at
your school about your stepdad?

Karlie My mom was at all those sessions with me.

Caroline Do you think the counsellor would have
believed you if you had told her?

Karlie She was totally on my mom's side, I thought. She
was always telling me to think about how my actions
hurt *her*.

Caroline Was there anyone else you could have trusted?

Karlie shakes her head.

You were still pretty active at your church then, right?

Karlie So was my stepdad. He was a deacon. Everybody
thought he was like the perfect fucking Christian.

Peter Language.

Karlie Everyone there worshipped him, practically. He
did adult Bible study. He did Promise Keepers. He did
Mrs Reeder when her husband was out of town on a
canoe trip –

Caroline Now now . . .

Peter (*overlapping*) Come on.

Beat.

Karlie He did Promise Keepers.

Caroline Is that part of why you turned your back on religion? Because in your experience the people in the church weren't living up to its ideals?

Karlie That and it's a myth about a completely made-up narcissistic asshole –

Peter Language.

Caroline (*overlapping*) Attitude.

Karlie Yes. That's why I left the church.

Caroline Okay. That's probably what the judge will ask you. Then – we should see what else we can work into your therapy sessions.

Takes a drink of coffee. It's cold. She pours herself more from the carafe.

I love this bottomless cup of coffee.

Karlie It's crap coffee.

Caroline It's okay if you keep it hot.
Now, if I were Gina I would ask you if you ever told Peter about your stepdad.

Karlie No.

Caroline Why not?

Karlie I was . . .

Pause.

Caroline What?

Karlie I don't know.

Caroline Ashamed?

Karlie Sure.

Caroline Were you afraid he would reject you if he found out?

Karlie Sure. Whatever.

Caroline It's really common for victims of sexual abuse to feel they were responsible for the abuse.

Even if you're being abused, sometimes you're still aroused . . .

So, if you feel like you enjoyed it on any level . . .

It's very common, for kids, to feel that they were asking for it or somehow deserved it. Or if it happened repeatedly, that they were at fault for not stopping it. So you might have felt like you couldn't even tell Peter.

Karlie That sounds good.

Beat.

Caroline How are things at the Auto Zone?

Peter You know, it doesn't completely suck. And my dad is a mechanic?

Caroline I didn't know that.

Peter He taught me some stuff, before, you know, he completely absconded. And went to jail. And then showed up at our door last year with a can of macadamia nuts.

Karlie His dad buys food at the dollar store.

Peter In LaCrosse.

Karlie It's still a fucking dollar store.

Peter But he's in another state.

Karlie stares at him.

I'm just saying, he lives in Wisconsin. He's only been to visit twice. That's why he brings presents.

Karlie From the dollar store.

Caroline What was he in jail for?

Karlie (*scoffing*) Kiting cheques.

Peter Do you want it to be something worse?

Karlie It's lame.

Peter Anyway – my dad's a mechanic, and some of the stuff he told me when I was a wee lad has come back. But mostly the guys at the counter just hand me numbers and I go get shit off the shelves.

Mock enthusiasm.

But I'm hoping to advance!

Caroline Good.

If there were anything else about Karlie. That we can come up with. For Gina. That would be helpful.

Peter Like what?

Caroline Physical stuff. Like, is she shy about being naked in front of you?

Peter She doesn't parade around, but I've definitely seen her business.

Caroline No. You should say she *is* shy.

Peter Right. Sorry.

Caroline When you do show her affection, does she seem relaxed with it? Or does she seem to physically tense up.

Peter doesn't answer. This sounds familiar.

Like when you hug her, does she hug you back? Or does she pull away?

Peter Um, you know. I don't know.

Caroline Does she initiate sex?

This hits a nerve.

Peter (*beat. Lies*) Yes.

Beat.

Or, I'm sorry. No. Right?

Caroline Right. Good. You should bring that up, too, with Gina.
   At your next session. Okay? We've only got two weeks until our next court date. So the more we can work into Gina's reports the better.

Peter Uh-huh.

Caroline Look, guys, I know this is hard, but you're doing great. Just . . . stay strong for Luna.

Her phone rings.

I gotta get this. Sorry.

Answers it.

Mrs Del Rosario? . . . Thanks for calling back. Can you hold on one second?

To Peter and Karlie.

You're seeing Luna on Tuesday?

Peter Yuh-huh.

Caroline Great then. I'll see you then.

As she goes, on the phone.

Hi. Sorry about that. I've been trying to reach Lourdes and I wondered if you'd heard from her . . .

Caroline exits. Pause.

Peter She didn't eat her pie.

Beat.

Here's something funny I noticed: is that when the lady is telling us how to talk to Gina about this made-up thing with your stepdad? Like, it stops feeling made-up, kind of, because a lot of what she's telling us to say is actually true. About us. Have you noticed that?

Karlie No.

Peter It's funny. Though. Because when she first asked you what happened to you when you were fifteen, and you were like, 'Nothing,' I believed you.
    And then she suggested that this might have happened, and you said, 'Sure.' But not like, 'Sure it happened.' Like, 'Sure, I'll go along with that, if that's what it takes.' So I've been operating under the assumption this whole time that it was made up, but it's kinda uncanny how not made up it feels –

Karlie It was only once.

Beat.

Peter Oh yeah?

Karlie In his car. It was only once. So it's no big deal.

Peter I think it's the definition of a big deal.
    How come I didn't know?

Karlie Who wants to know shit like that?

Beat.

Seriously. Who wants to know?

End of scene.

*Caroline's office, the next day. She is showing Cliff and
Pastor Jay in. She probably has to move some files off
some chairs so they can sit.*

Cliff I thought you could answer the Pastor's questions
because I can't, because I don't know anything about this.

Caroline Yes you do. It's Minor Child: Luna Gale.

Cliff But have I seen this new case plan?

Caroline No. But it's totally standard.

Looking out the door.

Should I get a chair for Cindy?

Cliff She's not coming.

Pastor Jay (*overlapping*) She doesn't know I'm here.

Caroline Then this feels inappropriate to me.

Cliff It's fine. Let's just answer the Pastor's questions if
we can. This alleged abuse happened when?

Caroline When Karlie was fifteen.

Cliff Four years ago. And the stepfather isn't in the
house any more.

Pastor Jay Martin's living in Missouri, last we heard.

Cliff Then how is he a threat to Luna?

Caroline That's not it. It's that Cindy didn't believe
Karlie when she told her about the abuse.
    She put her in physical and emotional jeopardy. And
until she deals with her non-offender issues, we can't
recommend placing Luna with her and we have to put
a hold on the TPR.

Cliff I don't see it.

Caroline That's the standard case plan.

Cliff It's a judgement call. There's no immediate threat.

Caroline I'm going by the book, Cliff.

She opens a drawer and pulls out a spiral-bound manual. To Pastor Jay.

Literally. We have a manual –

Holds the manual out to Pastor Jay.

If you want to look at the Sexual Abuse section it's the teal tab there . . .

Pastor Jay doesn't take the manual.

There's nothing, you know, explicit in it . . .

Pastor Jay Caroline, do you not like Cindy?

Caroline I don't have any feelings toward her one way or the other.

Pastor Jay You're not down on her because of her faith?

Caroline No. Where did that come from?

Pastor Jay Cindy says you laughed at her and made some joke about Jesus being a personal trainer?

Cliff You did what?

Caroline No, no. I misheard something, was all. It doesn't have anything to do with this. This is standard. Procedure.

Well, I can show you.

Holds out the book.

There are boxes. If this, then that . . .

Looks at a page.

86

Like, 'Does non-offending caregiver fully believe that the abuse occurred?' If no, then 'Non-offending caregiver has issues that should be addressed.' That's the box I checked for Cindy. In my mind. Not on the paper.

Neither man responds. Beat. She reads again.

'Was the non-offending caregiver sexually abused as a child?'

Cliff 'Is the non-offending caregiver a crazy Christian?'

Pastor Jay What's that?

Beat. Caroline stares hard at the manual.

Caroline That's not . . . I'm not . . . there's not a box for that.

Her cell phone rings. She kind of jumps on it.

Cliff Don't answer that.

Caroline It's Lourdes. I need to talk to her –

Cliff You can call her back.

Caroline She never answers.

Cliff It can wait. Silence it.

Beat. Caroline silences her phone.

Pastor Jay What is your faith, Caroline?

Caroline That's such an inappropriate question.

Cliff I'd be curious to know that, too.

Beat.

Caroline Look, I know what you're accusing me of and all I can say is, my personal feelings about Christianity or any other religion do not factor into my decision-making on this or any other case. I work with Christians and churches all the time. Catholic services. Lutheran Children's Network. Whatever works. That's my motto.

Stands.

So, gentlemen, if you'll excuse me, I need to get back to work now.

Neither man moves.

Cliff Well, since you're not biased, and it is a judgement call, why don't we just say that this isn't a factor in Cindy's plan and she's not required to undergo any treatment.

Pastor Jay Terrific.

Caroline No.

Cliff No?

Caroline She has to deal with what she did to her daughter. I'm not giving her Luna so she can screw her up like she screwed up Karlie.

Pastor Jay Cindy did all she could for Karlie –

Cliff (*overlapping*) You mean by being a crazy Christian?

Pastor Jay Why do you keep saying 'crazy Christian'?

Cliff I don't know. It's something I heard once, somewhere. From somebody.

Beat.

Caroline Okay, I do have a bias.

Cliff This is unfortunate –

Caroline But it's not the one you think.
    Can I please just explain it to you please? Pastor. Can I close the door? So we can do this in private?

Cliff I don't think you need to close the door.

Caroline What I have to say is personal.

Pastor Jay She can close the door, can't she?

Cliff I'm staying.

Caroline I'm not asking you to go.

Caroline closes the door. Takes a breath.

Cindy reminds me of my mom. Is the thing.

Cliff Your mother was a Christian?

Caroline My mom was an alcoholic.
I'm going to keep this short.
She was a very miserable person. And every night, she would drink Scotch until she passed out on the couch.
My dad went to bed at nine o'clock because he had to get up at four. He drove a milk truck . . .

Beat.

But also, he got up early so he could come up to my room. While my mom was on the couch. And, you know . . .

Stops.

Pastor Jay He abused you?

Caroline Off and on from seventh grade through high school. I thought at the time that my mom didn't give him the love he needed, so it was up to me to –

Stops.

But now I know, she drank because she knew what was happening and she didn't want to face it.

Pastor Jay I'm so sorry, Caroline.

Cliff (*rote*) That's tough.

Caroline could kill Cliff.

Caroline (*to Pastor Jay*) Thank you.

Pastor Jay Well, she must have been very lonely. Your mother.

Caroline She was.

Pastor Jay And you must have felt abandoned.

Caroline I did.
   Or not completely. I guess. I had a really great counsellor. In high school. And she saw, like just from how I acted – she saw that something was wrong and she got me through graduation and into college and I didn't become an alcoholic or an abusive parent. Or anything.

Pastor Jay You became a social worker.

Caroline I set out to help kids like me.

Pastor Jay Bless you. For that.

Caroline I'm not perfect, though.
   When I found out that Karlie said she had been abused, I got really angry. I know what it is to grow up with a mother who doesn't protect you, or believe in you. I know how worthless that can make you feel. So I think Cindy should have to face up to what happened. Luna aside, she needs to acknowledge that she hurt Karlie.
   And that's my bias. That's what I have against Cindy.

Cliff It's not that she's a crazy Christian.

Caroline Would you stop saying that?

Pastor Jay Or explain why you're saying it? Cliff?

   Beat.

Caroline It's because I said it. Earlier. I said it. But all I meant is, I think Cindy loves Jesus more than she loves her daughter. The way my mom loved Scotch more than she loved me.

Cliff I don't think that's what you meant.

Caroline It is but I didn't want to tell you this thing about me because I don't like telling people about it

90

because it's gross. And I don't know you. Okay? So I said it in a stupid, inarticulate way but that's what I was trying to say. I don't feel like Cindy loves Karlie the way she should. That's all.

Pastor Jay But what if – Caroline? What if Cindy has a different kind of love for Karlie. Something even stronger than a mother's love. Have you ever thought of that?

Caroline No.

Pastor Jay It's not that Cindy loves Jesus more than she loves Karlie. It's that she wants Karlie to feel Jesus' love more than her own. This is hard for anybody to understand who doesn't know that love yet. But when you know it . . .

It's the answer to every problem that exists, and when you feel it? You want to share it with the people you love the most. It's the greatest gift you can give them and if they resist it, you get so frustrated. It just –

Can't articulate it.

Cliff knows. Cliff ministers. He's an ambassador.

Caroline What is Cliff an ambassador to?

Cliff It's not important.

Pastor Jay TGIW.

Caroline Thank God It's Wednesday?

Pastor Jay (*laughs*) Teaching God's Infinite Wisdom. It's a men's group –

Caroline Is that how you two know each other?

Cliff The pastor spoke at a conference I attended once. We're not friends.

Pastor Jay I consider you a friend.

Cliff But we're not . . . right now this is professional.

Pastor Jay Sure. Sure. But Caroline, do you see what I'm saying? About Cindy and Karlie? I know, how Cindy comes across. She's a handful. High-strung and wound-tight, as my daddy used to say.

But it's only because of how very much she wants Karlie to feel Jesus' love. Just like I would like you to be able to feel Jesus' love for you.

This is a terrible burden you're carrying, a terrible shame around what happened to you as a girl. I could lift it from you if you'd let me try.

Would you let me pray with you and for you, Caroline? Would you let me do that?

Beat. Caroline and Cliff regard each other.

Cliff? What if we both prayed with Caroline?

Cliff I think it's up to Caroline if we pray or not.

Caroline Do you want me to pray?

Cliff Do you have something against it?

Caroline Not if you don't.

Pastor Jay Terrific. Caroline, why don't you come around here.

He moves the chairs so they can all stand together. Caroline and Cliff, still eyeing each other, move in.

Cliff, I'll put my hand on Caroline.

He puts his hand on Caroline's shoulder, facing her. Cliff gets behind the Pastor and puts his hand on his shoulder. In other words, Cliff knows exactly what to do. The two men bow their heads and Caroline follows.
Pastor Jay prays in a familiar way. His voice is gentle, kind.

Lord Jesus, we need You to look upon all of us here this morning, but especially our new friend, Caroline. Lord,

Caroline has endured too much pain in this world. Pain she didn't ask for. Pain she definitely didn't deserve. She was born to parents who turned away from You. And in their exile, they turned on her. And they did the most terrible thing that parents can do: they made her feel unloved and unwanted.

But Caroline is neither of those things, Lord. You know that. I know that. She is a loved and wanted child, a precious child. Because she is Your child. You brought her into this world and You love her and she is perfect in Your eyes.

He makes Caroline make eye contact with him.

You are perfect, Caroline. You know that, don't you?

Pause. Caroline nods. Quiet.

You are beautiful and you are perfect.

Bows his head again. Caroline might cry.

Jesus, take control of the throne of Caroline's life. Make her the person You want her to be. Fill her with Your love and Your spirit and erase the pain and the unearned shame she carries. Make her whole, again, Lord. And bring her peace.

Bring her peace.

Pause.

Thank You, Jesus, for dying on the cross for our sins. Thank You for giving us eternal life, and eternal love.

Beat.

In Lord Jesus' name.

Pastor Jay *and* **Cliff** Amen.

They break the chain. Pastor Jay considers Caroline.

Pastor Jay How long has it been since you prayed?

Caroline A long time.

Pastor Jay How did it feel?

Caroline I don't know.

Pastor Jay That sounds about right.

But here's the thing: God cannot love you more than He does this very instant. He will sneak up on you. And He'll give you His love whether you want it or not. So be prepared.

So where are we with this whole thing? With Cindy? Can we forgive her her past mistakes and move on knowing she only wants the best for her family?

Caroline I think I should talk it over with Cliff.

Cliff I think Caroline knows what's fair and what isn't.

Pastor Jay That's all we ask. Caroline, thank you for talking with me today. I so appreciate it. I know how swamped you are. And may you be blessed in your good work.

Caroline Okay.

Pastor Jay I'll see you both soon, I hope.

Cliff Goodbye, Pastor. Thank you.

Pastor Jay goes. Cliff closes the door.

You called her a crazy Christian because she believed in the second coming, not because she didn't love her daughter enough. You're clearly persecuting this woman. This is it. I'm calling Des Moines and – seniority or not – you are out –

Caroline You made me pray.

Cliff No I didn't.

Caroline You're my supervisor. You pressured me into doing it. I only did it to save my job –

Cliff You only did it to show me up!

94

Caroline And you pressured me into recommending the concurrent permanency plan because Cindy's a Christian and she's a friend of your pastor pal –

Cliff He's not my 'pastor pal' –

Caroline The bias is yours. It is your pro-Christian bias. That you're using against me. This is a hostile workplace –

Cliff Because of you!

Caroline You asked me what my faith was! So try to fire me. Try to lay me off or even just take me off the case and I will go to the IWC –

Cliff Oh come on!

Caroline (*overlapping*) And they will file a workplace discrimination claim and I won't take arbitration. I'll insist on a full hearing in front of the commission and it'll be so ugly, even if you win, you're never gonna make regional director. This is going to haunt you just like that thing with Mimi is haunting me and you're gonna be stuck here for ever. With me!

Cliff You're insane.

Caroline Like a fox.

Cliff That's not even the expression!

Caroline (*shudders*) 'He sneaks up and he gives you his love whether you want it or not.'
　　Jesus Christ. God is just like my fucking father.

End of scene.

The visitation room at DHS, the following Wednesday. It is a sad, harshly lit room with some very tired plastic chairs, toys and wooden jigsaw puzzles. The dominating feature is the two-way mirror on the upstage wall.

Luna is asleep in a stroller. We can't see her.

Cindy sits with the baby. She is rocking the stroller back and forth and humming, tunelessly. Peter enters in his work clothes.

Peter Oh. Hey.

Cindy Peter. Hello.

Peter Am I early or something?

Cindy Where's Karlie?

Peter She couldn't come.

Cindy (*smirks*) Right.

Peter Somebody called in sick and her boss said if she left she'd get fired. Where's Ms Cox?

Cindy She had an emergency phone call. Her supervisor said I could wait with Luna. I need to talk to Karlie.

Peter She doesn't want to talk to you.

Cindy Tell her she has to stop all this. They're going to make me go to this counsellor and lie. They don't care what the real story is. Pastor Jay even talked to them and they wouldn't even listen to him. Our lawyer says maybe we can sue. But the next court date is Wednesday –

Peter (*overlapping*) Wednesday. I know because I'll be there, because she's my daughter, actually. Can I please – can I sit with her please? This is supposed to be my time with her.

Cindy She's almost asleep.

Peter I'm not going to wake her up.

Cindy moves. Peter takes her place and rocks the stroller. He starts humming the Oklahoma Sooners' fight song. Pause.

96

Cindy Why does Karlie hate me, Peter?

Peter Why do you hate her?

Cindy I don't hate her. She hates me. This thing she said happened, it didn't happen.

Peter It did. Actually.

Cindy But she never told me anything about Martin doing anything. Or maybe she dreamed she told me, but she didn't tell me.

Peter You still knew. You knew all sorts of shit. You knew, like, how Martin was always commenting on Karlie's clothes and telling her how to wear her hair and talking about how 'developed' she was.

Cindy We both wanted her to keep her hair long.

Peter You were his fourth wife. You knew.

Cindy I didn't.

Peter You knew right after it happened.

Cindy After what happened?

Peter sighs.

Peter It was in May? And you were at church and it was after services and Martin was driving Karlie home and you were staying to do something with a butterfly garden? That somebody donated?

Cindy A butterfly garden?

Peter That somebody donated for some lady who died and her brother carved a rock or something?

Cindy Jenny McMannus' memorial garden?

Peter You were putting in a rock.

Cindy Her brother made a memorial stone carving. He carves things in stone with a laser.

Peter stares at her.

What does this have to do with anything?

Peter And Martin said he'd drive Karlie home and you were getting a ride with somebody else.

Cindy I don't know about that.

Peter And he drove Karlie, he said, 'Let's don't go straight home, let's just drive out toward Mount Vernon,' because it was a warm day and he drove her out some farm road he knew that he said was a shortcut to Mount Vernon and it cut across a corn field and then it turned and went down a hill into some woods where there was a stream –

Cindy This is a long story.

Peter I just heard it so the details are fresh, okay?

Cindy But why are you telling it?

Peter To show you why you should have known. Isn't that what you wanted to know?

During this, he stops rocking Luna.

It went down into these woods and then it dead-ended. Nobody could see them. It was like two miles down there and Karlie was laughing at Martin because she thought he was lost because it was a dead-end road. And he turned off the engine and he said, 'Don't laugh at me. I don't want you to laugh at me any more.' And he unbuckled his pants and pulled them down and pulled down his underwear too, because he wore briefs, right? Not boxers.

Cindy doesn't answer. She closes her eyes.

He did. And Karlie said it was so weird, she thought maybe he just needed to take a piss or something. But before she could figure it out he basically shoved himself over and pulled her on to his lap. She was wearing a skirt you bought her at Marshall's and he pushed it up and yanked down her panties and then he put his hand on her back and pushed her into the windshield – pushed her up with one hand so he could jam his dick in her from behind and he did. He started fucking her as hard as he could. Karlie put her hands up on the windshield but her forehead kept hitting the glass anyway. Karlie said for like weeks after that whenever she got in the car she could see her handprints on the inside of the windshield.

And she was a virgin and there was bleeding. She bled all the way home and when they got home you were already there and you were in the kitchen when they came inside and you didn't ask where they'd been. Or what took them so long. You saw them come in and you saw whatever you saw on their faces and you didn't say a word and they didn't say a word and you watched Karlie walk through the kitchen and down the hall and when she got to her room she took off her clothes and she had bled through her panties and there was a blood stain on the back of her skirt. Her skirt was yellow and there was a huge honking red stain on the back.

Cindy She didn't tell me.

Peter Did she really need to tell you?

Long pause. Peter resumes rocking Luna's stroller and humming the Sooners' fight song.

Cindy What is that song?

Beat.

Peter It's the Sooners' fight song.

Cindy What?

Peter The Oklahoma Sooners. I don't know why. She likes it.

Cindy This is Iowa.

Peter But I don't know the Iowa fight song.

Cindy It was lonely.

Peter What?

Cindy I was lonely.
  You don't know yet. How lonely you can get –

The door opens and Caroline enters.

Caroline Cliff?

To Cindy.

What are you doing here?

Cindy (*points at Peter*) She admitted it to him. She never told me.

Caroline doesn't hear her.

Caroline (*to the mirror*) Are you in there?

Peter Somebody's watching?

Caroline (*to the mirror*) Cliff.

Cindy (*overlapping*) Then he heard –

A door in the hallway opens and Cliff comes out and into the doorway of the visiting room.

Cliff Did you find Lourdes?

Caroline She wasn't in the emergency room, she was outside it in a car. Her sister's boyfriend's car. He drove her there and left her outside in the car.

Cliff Is she dead?

Caroline She overdosed.

Cliff She's dead?

Caroline Yes. She's dead.

Cliff Did you call Mrs Del Rosario?

Caroline No.

Cliff Do that then.

Caroline stares at him for a moment, then pushes past him, exiting.
Cliff looks at Peter and Cindy.

Cindy (*to Cliff*) You heard what he said. She never told me. She never told me, so I never knew.

End of scene.

SCENE SIX

The break room at the courthouse. Early morning. Karlie, dressed very respectably, is waiting. She nervously chews on a fingernail. She is jumpy.
Peter enters. He is also respectably dressed.

Peter The guy said we're third on the docket. I didn't see Ms Cox anywhere.

Peter sees Karlie is chewing on a nail. He takes her hand away from her face.

Stop doing that.

Karlie I'm nervous.

Peter You don't have to be.

Karlie How can I not be? This whole thing is nerve-racking.

Peter But I seriously think we have a chance. I seriously think we could go home with Luna today.

Karlie You'll jinx it if you say it.

She starts chewing on her nail again.

Peter You know, since we're in the courthouse, why don't we see about getting a marriage licence? Like after we talk to the judge. I think we should totally do that.

Karlie You want to get married?

Peter I know the institution is meaningless and we said we'd never do it, but I kinda feel like we should. Since we're getting Luna back.

Karlie Don't say it or you'll jinx it.

Peter I have a good feeling, though.

Karlie It's not real.

Peter Not if you don't believe it's real.

Caroline enters. She carries a file.

Hey. We're ready.

Caroline I need to talk to Karlie. Alone. Why don't you wait upstairs?

Peter What is it?

Caroline Go upstairs and if you see Gina, tell her to wait for me outside the courtroom.

Peter We were thinking we'd get married.

Caroline What?

Peter Since we're at the courthouse.

Caroline Peter, this is not –

Karlie Just go!

Peter I'll wait for you upstairs, okay?

He goes.

Caroline When did you do it?

Karlie stares at her. Caroline pulls out a sheet of paper.

It's on your results –

Karlie After we saw you at the restaurant. That girl who I got a bump from the first time? She still works there. Duh.

Caroline Does Peter know?

Karlie He doesn't *know*, know. But he knows something's up.

Caroline He loves you.

Karlie Too much! You know?
   He only did meth because he saw how good it made me feel and he knew if he didn't feel as good as I did, I'd leave him.

Caroline That is . . . makes no sense.

Karlie It does, though. Have you ever smoked it?

Caroline No.

Karlie It's like – it's like – it fills you out.

Caroline Fills you out?

Karlie Like every bit of space?

She starts over.

Like you are entirely peaceful and down with everything on the planet. Like every bit of you. You are so . . . like . . . all your self-doubt disappears because it doesn't even make any sense any more that you would doubt anything you do because why would you? Because you're perfect.
   You can do no wrong.

Caroline I'm sorry.

Karlie Don't be. I'm fucked up right now.

Beat.

Caroline So. Since your urinalysis was positive, and your mother refuses to get treatment –

Karlie She does?

Caroline Yes.

Karlie So you were right. You knew she wouldn't.

Caroline Yeah.

Karlie You were right about my stepdad, too. Did you know that?

Caroline I didn't *know* know.

Karlie But you guessed.

Caroline I had a gut feeling.

Karlie Because I just exude, like, victimhood?

Caroline Because I've seen it before. A million times.

Karlie And here I thought I was special.

The loss hits Caroline.

Caroline You are! You all are. But there are so many of you and you just keep coming and I can't seem to slow it down so I can figure out how to save you or even just . . . keep you alive long enough to . . . have a life. That's all. Just have a life.

Beat.

Karlie I'm sorry?

Caroline tries to compose herself.

Caroline So since your mom's no longer an option, we have to place Luna in foster care until we figure out – either . . . If I can get you into rehab would you go?

Karlie Sure.

Caroline If you can stay sober for a year, you can petition to have her back.
 There's no reason for you to come upstairs. Why don't you wait down here?

Karlie What about Peter?

Caroline Peter's not an option as long as he's living with you.

Karlie What?

Caroline Peter can't have custody of Luna as long as he's living with you.

Karlie I only meant . . . I only meant . . . who was going to tell him the bad news?

Caroline Oh. Me. I'll tell him.

Karlie Thank you.

Caroline It's the least I can do.

Karlie It is.

> *Caroline considers, then exits.*
> *Beat. Karlie gets up, throws away hers and Peter's coffee cups. She goes back to the table. She looks at her wrist but she doesn't have a watch.*
> *Long pause.*
> *She picks up a napkin. Then she searches in her bag for a pen. Eventually she finds one.*
> *She tries to write a note on the napkin but the pen isn't working. She scribbles on the napkin, trying to get it to work. It doesn't.*
> *Whispers.*

Stupid fucking . . .

She gives up and throws the pen and the napkin in the trash.

She exits in the opposite direction from Caroline and Peter.

End of scene.

SCENE SEVEN

A month later. The visiting room.

Luna is asleep in her stroller, in the visiting room. No one else is there.

There is a gift bag on the floor.

Cliff enters the visiting room. He looks at the stroller, then looks directly at the mirror.

Cliff Are you in there?

Cliff goes to the mirror. Caroline, on the other side, knocks on the glass. Cliff motions for her to come into the room.

Caroline exits the viewing room, and enters the visiting room.

You don't want to sit with the baby?

Caroline I could see her.

Cliff Do you not like children?

Caroline I love children. That's why I never had them.

Beat.

Cliff When does the memorial start?

Caroline Mrs Del Rosario said we could get there any time after four. She's making empenadas. She said Lourdes loved them.

Cliff What about her dorm room?

Caroline I went and cleaned it out.

Cliff You did?

Caroline She'd stopped going to classes her third or fourth week, I guess? She was just pretending to go. Her room mate was completely clueless.

Cliff Have we heard from the sister?

Caroline Why should we?

Beat.

Cliff Lourdes was an adult.

Caroline I know.

Cliff There wasn't anything else you could have done.

Beat.

Caroline Are you trying to make me feel better?

He doesn't answer. But he is.

Cliff So my big news is, I'm leaving DHS.

Caroline You are?

Cliff Pastor Jay and some of his colleagues have decided to start a children's services consulting firm –

Caroline What in God's name is that?

Cliff – for couples interested in becoming foster parents and for foster parents who are considering adoption –

Caroline Oh.

Cliff – to help people navigate the system more effectively.

Caroline To help the Christians get all the little poor children. Smart.

Beat.

Cliff I'm not going to argue with you, or take exception to the fact that you openly mock my deepest beliefs –

Caroline Okay.

Cliff – because once I leave, I'm hoping I'll never see you again –

Caroline Fair enough.

Cliff – and also in your own insane way it turns out you were right, about . . .

Gestures towards Luna.

Caroline Luna Gale. Minor child.

Beat.

Cliff They're going to appoint an interim director until they can hire someone new in January. They've asked me for a recommendation –

Caroline And you recommended me?

Cliff You can't have that job. For good reason. So I recommended they promote you to district coordinator.

Caroline District coordinator?

Cliff I told them you're suffering from extreme burn-out but that you still have a wealth of expertise and experience that they can use and you should be a district coordinator.

Caroline That's nothing but budgets, and –

Cliff It's nothing but administration. You wouldn't have cases any more. You'd just –

Caroline Go to meetings.

Cliff Go to meetings. Write reports. Kick back until your retirement.

Beat.

Caroline I wouldn't have any more cases.

Cliff You wouldn't be responsible for any more children. No.

Stands.

You can thank me later.

Caroline I can thank you now.

Silence.

Cliff I assume we're taking separate cars to Lourdes' memorial service.

Caroline You assume correctly, yes.

Cliff Then I'll see you there.

He goes.
Caroline walks over to Luna and looks into the stroller.

Caroline Hey, sleepy. Look at you. Who do you belong to? Who to you belong to, huh?

Peter enters.

Hey.

Peter Hey.

Caroline Where's your dad?

Peter He dropped me off and ran back over to Target. We realised the diapers I had are probably too small.

Caroline picks up the diaper bag hanging on the stroller.

Caroline I got you a starter kit. It's got diapers, formula –

Peter We got all that. Except the diapers I had were from four to six.

Caroline Take it anyway. It's the least we can do.

Peter You know, I don't want it. No offence but it's got that welfare smell.

Caroline I understand.
  There's forms.

Peter Of course.

She opens the file, pulls out some papers, hands one to Peter.

Caroline This is yours to keep. This is the number for the DHS in LaCrosse. Your caseworker's direct line is here. You need to call her by Tuesday –

Peter Okay.

Caroline This is the change of jurisdiction form. Sign that and give it to me, then keep that copy for yourself.

Peter signs.

Peter So is somebody in La Crosse expecting me? Like do they know my whole story and stuff?

Caroline I faxed over your file –

Peter I just . . . want to know, if Karlie comes back, is there some plan for how to . . .?

He can't find the words.

Caroline She'd have to petition for custody, in Wisconsin. And go through their system. If she comes back. I assume you've been calling her . . .?

Peter Her phone's disconnected. I was thinking . . . I hope she calls me first and doesn't just go to our apartment because then she'll think I just left.
  If she comes back.

Caroline I'm sorry you can't stay here, but the judge isn't going to give you custody on your own. Your dad has to be the primary guardian. And he's got a good job. You can't ask him to move –

Peter I know.

Caroline And you get to be with your daughter.

Peter I know.

Caroline Which is what I think Karlie had in mind.

Beat. Peter is profoundly sad.

You know, you never know what's going to happen –

Peter I don't need any words of wisdom. Okay? She left. Is all.

Beat.

Caroline So I want to give Luna this present. If you don't mind.

She hands him the gift bag. He pulls out a teddy bear – the same as the one Caroline gave to Lourdes. It's white, with a red, satin heart.

Peter Gosh.

Caroline I know. It's hideous.

We usually give them out to kids when they age out of foster care but – that's not going very well and I thought, what if we mixed it up?

What if, instead of a perfunctory, meaningless gesture of hope at the end of the story, we tried –

Stops.

Peter A perfunctory, meaningless gesture at the beginning?

Caroline What if I said to Luna, 'I believe you're going to be okay. So I'm going to go ahead and give this to you now'?

Peter How can you say she's going to be okay?

Caroline Because I believe in you.
Because I believe that you're a very, very good person.

Peter If you say so.

Caroline I do.

Beat. He accepts it.

Peter Okay.

Caroline (*indicating the stroller*) Can I put this in here?

Peter Sure.

She puts the bear in the stroller.

My dad's gonna call when he gets here –

Caroline I understand. I have to go anyway. Drive safe, okay?

Peter Okay.

Caroline Take care.

Caroline exits. Luna makes a fussy noise. Peter goes to her, and rocks her stroller. He begins to hum the Oklahoma Sooners' fight song. Then he begins to make up words to go along with the tune.

Peter Luna Buna, Luna Buna.
Luna Buna. Luna Buna.

Pause. Then he takes the bear out of the stroller and gently puts it aside.
He sings again, to the same tune.

Luna Buna. You're my Luna.
My little Luna. And I love you.

End of play.